Sonia

Sonia

My Story

SONIA O'SULLIVAN
with TOM HUMPHRIES

PENGUIN
IRELAND

PENGUIN IRELAND

Published by the Penguin Group
Penguin Ireland, 25 St Stephen's Green, Dublin 2, Ireland
(a division of Penguin Books Ltd)
Penguin Books Ltd, 80 Strand, London WC2R ORL, England
Penguin Group (USA) Inc., 375 Hudson Street, New York, New York 10014, USA
Penguin Group (Australia), 250 Camberwell Road, Camberwell, Victoria 3124, Australia
(a division of Pearson Australia Group Pty Ltd)
Penguin Group (Canada), 90 Eglinton Avenue East, Suite 700, Toronto, Ontario, Canada M4P 2Y3
(a division of Pearson Penguin Canada Inc.)
Penguin Books India Pvt Ltd, 11 Community Centre, Panchsheel Park, New Delhi – 110 017, India
Penguin Group (NZ), 67 Apollo Drive, Rosedale, North Shore 0632, New Zealand
(a division of Pearson New Zealand Ltd)
Penguin Books (South Africa) (Pty) Ltd, 24 Sturdee Avenue, Rosebank, Johannesburg 2196, South Africa

Penguin Books Ltd, Registered Offices: 80 Strand, London WC2R ORL, England

www.penguin.com

First published 2008

1

Copyright © Sonia O'Sullivan, 2008

The moral right of the author has been asserted

Set in 12/14.75 pt Postscript Monotype Bembo
Typeset by Rowland Phototypesetting Ltd, Bury St Edmunds, Suffolk
Printed in Great Britain by Clays Ltd, St Ives plc

A CIP catalogue record for this book is available from the British Library

ISBN 978-1-844-88163-5

www.greenpenguin.co.uk

For Ciara and Sophie

It's warm here in Barcelona. A gentle evening breeze is fanning us through the formalities. The sky is the colour of bruised plums. I'm hopping from foot to foot. Impatient. Edgy. I hate waiting. We all do.

Strange thing. All this noise, but you can hear your heart beat. All these people, but you are alone. All this preparation, but you aren't ready.

I hear my name called. At last. I step forward and give a little wave. Hi! On a screen way above where I am standing a giant version of myself steps forward at the same time and does the same thing. Half the people on the planet watch the wave. Then another name is called. The girl beside me steps towards the camera and waves to half the world. Best not to think about what it all means.

Anyway, you boil it down and it means just the same thing it always has. Racing.

It was always an adventure, always something to get my pulse going. As a kid I raced from lamp post to lamp post on the walk home from school, trying to get from start to finish quicker than a car which I would randomly pick from the passing traffic. I raced friends through the gardens of Wilmount Park and up and down the hills of Cobh. Racing. Racing. Racing. Always loved it.

We used to have this game as kids. Two of us would split up and walk to my house using different routes. The idea was to find out which way was the quickest. My way was always the quickest because as soon as I was out of sight I would run till my heart burst. We weren't cartographers. We were racers.

The first race I remember was for the Community Games. You got a lollipop if you won. Dipped your hand into a big box held out by Sister Rosario and got to pull out a lollipop. I busted a gut. The lollipop was good but the racing was its own reward.

I joined the athletics club so I could go to the discos. And then, so I could spare myself for racing, I pretended that I wasn't allowed to go to the discos. I wrapped myself up in cotton wool and kept myself for racing.

I raced in green fields through cowpats and dark mud, with a last-lap bell and a hysterical commentary sounding through my head. I graduated to racing on patchy tartan tracks and to the glamour of owning my own spikes. I washed those spikes by hand a million times between the races.

Places and races. Cobh. Dungarvan. Killenaule. Dublin. Villanova. Crystal Palace . . . here. Stepping stones. I kept doing the same thing; the races just got bigger. I just kept putting one foot in front of the other as quickly as I could and feeling the same thrill. Getting fast. Going fast. Going faster than anyone else. Keeping going. Racing.

So this is Barcelona. This is 1992. This is the Olympics. This is the final of the 3000 metres. More racing.

The names of the people in this race are called out. Patti Sue Plummer and Shelly Steely, two Americans. Yelena Romanova, Tetyana Dorovskikh and Yelena Kopytova, three girls who were once Soviet citizens but now since the break-up of the USSR are temporarily stateless, running for something called the Unified Team. Yvonne Murray of Scotland. Angela Chalmers of Canada. Alison Wyeth, my friend from England. Roberta Brunet of Italy. Margareta Keszeg of Romania. Marie-Pierre Duros of France. Me, Sonia O'Sullivan from Cobh.

When I ran in the fields as a kid I always ran barefoot, loving the feel of the wet grass on my skin. On the streets we'd ring on people's doorbells and go haring away helter-skelter through the gardens before they could answer. The others liked the danger. I liked the running.

That's how I got here. These are little things that journalists find interesting but on an Olympic starting line you are never the most interesting story.

On the line with me tonight is Patti Sue Plummer. She may be the most accident-prone runner in the world. Her record includes being knocked down by a taxi in Japan, catching pneumonia six times and being bitten by a dog before last year's World 1500-metre final. How Patti Sue managed to get here in one piece has to be a better story than mine.

Thirty-four of us qualified to compete at these Olympic Games. In the heats I watched Zola Budd Pieterse topple out. When Zola was seventeen she was running world records in apartheid-stained South Africa. After a tabloid newspaper campaigned to have her run for Britain she got the citizenship and then the famous white singlet, and I watched herself and Mary Decker Slaney tangle in the 1984 Olympic final, perhaps my clearest early Olympic memory. Now Zola is history. Fodder for the heats.

And there was Pauline Konga and Esther Kiplagat from Kenya. Married women couldn't even compete in Kenya until the late 1970s. It is a breakthrough for Kenyan culture for them even to be here. Shorts and hurdles are still frowned upon; these girls are the future though.

In my own heat, a slow one, the last-place finisher was a girl called Mirsada Buric. She is from Bosnia-Herzegovina and she trained for the race on the streets of Sarajevo. She was shot at twice by snipers. In June, along with other Muslim women, she was abducted by Serb militia and held for two weeks on a daily diet of tea and a slice of bread. All her running gear was stolen. This was six weeks before the Games.

And I think *I* have problems with the people who run athletics in Ireland!

This is the end of the road for us tonight. We started out, all of us, in some place racing for lollipops or for approval or for fun. Every Olympic journey started somewhere and survived because somebody who shared the passion was around long enough to help. We're here for a million different reasons perhaps, but mainly we are the ones who just kept on racing, kept on being addicted. Tonight, as our paths cross, we can say that all our journeys have led us to this landmark.

My first rival was a girl called Diane McCarthy. For a long time, to be as good as Diane McCarthy was all that I hoped for in running. Diane ran for a club called Grange Fermoy. She used to win everything there was to win.

I remember that they used to have these cross-country races in Fermoy. The Fermoy International. Miruts Yifter ('The Shifter') came and won the men's race on more than one occasion and we all gawked at him in appreciation. In Fermoy they would lay all the trophies out on a groaning table before the races and I would eye them up, knowing that the one I wanted was the one Diane would be going home with.

Diane would win all the time, until one day I beat her and just moved on. My father told me not to be cocky about it. 'There is always somebody will come along to beat you,' he said.

He was right. My next rival was Anita Philpott. She ran for North Cork. Father Liam Kelleher was the North Cork coach and they always had super squads, loads of good athletes. I was virtually by myself in Cobh.

Anita had it all, even headbands and a publicity machine. Father Kelleher ran *Marathon* magazine, which served as the in-house Bible for us Irish runners, and for years there was this whispered thing about how many pictures of Anita would appear in *Marathon* magazine and how many of me.

The rivalry was intense. At the time, in our grade the top three cross-country runners in Cork would have been the top three in Munster and the top three in Ireland.

I remember one time we were running in the Munster championship. We were under sixteen and this race was billed, among ourselves anyway, as Sonia *v.* Anita. The race was on the racecourse in Thurles. We were running around, myself and Anita, watching each other like hawks because, well, it was all about us surely, and then this girl Carmel McCarthy got ahead and just went and won the whole thing. Just like that. She made us look stupid! I was so disappointed that I can't remember if I was second or third.

We had loads of races during that rivalry. Anita won more than I did for a long time. We were never friends. We'd say hello but we were wary of each other. We both wanted to be top dog. We lived at opposite ends of the county and I never saw Anita unless we were competing or we were on the same team going away with the schools or county team. Back then the Irish schools team would have been a squad of eight, and four of them were from Cork. If you could win in Cork you could win in Munster and win in the All Irelands. One year the first, second and third in the Cork championships were the same one-two-three in the Nationals a while later. I think New York borrowed that line about 'If you can make it there, you can make it anywhere' from Cork.

I don't remember Anita as a schools competitor but rather as a rival on the club circuit. The age groups were different for schools, and cross-country races would be run off for the uneven ages before Christmas and for the even ages after Christmas. So at times we wouldn't run against each other for quite a while. I don't remember getting that stressed about always trying to beat the same person all the time, but I clearly remember the day when I beat Anita for the first time, so perhaps I was a little focused on it.

We went to the South Munster meeting in Cork. I was the only runner in the school racing at this level, and one of the teachers, Jim Hennessy, used to drive me to the races. He was one of the boys' teachers but he would always take an interest in my progress and give me a lift whenever it was needed. For some reason we were late and in a bit of a hurry, and we only got there ten minutes before the race was due to start. Maybe I was showing signs of being anxious, but he turned and said to me, 'You know what, Sonia, I have a good feeling about this today. I think you will beat this Philpott girl today.'

I listened and didn't say anything. We got there but there was no time to warm up. It was a windy day and I won by a fraction. I ran 4:35.1, and I won by the smallest margin possible. We were both given the same time but I was given the gold medal.

It's easy to say that when you are young it gives you a great boost to be told that you are going to win, but runners are fragile animals. All through my career I would need that sort of confidence, that feeling that I would win, that people expected me to win, that I was invincible.

★

5

I left the call room a while ago, telling myself over and over again that this could be the biggest thing I might ever do. Up the tunnel, and the warmth of the Barcelona evening hit my face as we stepped out on to the track, this little group of us, like performers in a huge circus. The stadium towering up all around us; and even though I had been out here for the heats the other day, the feeling of anticipation tonight made the place more daunting. I feel very small down here, a bit player in a major production.

Tonight on this line in this corner of a stadium in a foreign city I don't feel invincible but I feel full of adventure. Forty-eight hours ago, the heats seemed worse, more of an ordeal. I spent most of the summer at home in Ireland and I had let the talk and the speculation about the Olympics get into my bloodstream. Will ya win, Sonia? Of course ya will, girl! On Friday, when the heats finally came around, I was a wreck. I couldn't eat anything all day but plain rice with a pinch of salt.

I was shaky and the day seemed to drag and drag. I spent the afternoon writing postcards. In a way they proved to myself that I was here. I'M AT THE OLYMPICS! Perhaps I really should have been trying to convince myself that I was in the Mardyke or at Thurles racecourse or some other familiar spot.

There's a kind of innocence to me being here, even though I have done four years in college in America. Barcelona seemed to loom on the horizon for ages before I got here. It seemed like a shimmering city in the distance. So Sean Kennedy, my coach from at home, suggested a year ago that I should travel here and just have a look around and familiarize myself with the place so that I wouldn't feel like a wide-eyed tourist when I got to the Olympics. So I did just that. I flew into Madrid for some reason and, because I had a few hours to kill before my connection, I went outside and (God, this is embarrassing!) lay down in the sun. By the time I got up my face looked like a red traffic light. But I got to Barcelona and I got to know the Olympic city.

My heat was the last of the evening on Friday and it was slow, slow, slow. The previous heat, the second of three, had been a quick one and a whole slew of runners had qualified out of it. I

6

wasn't sure if we were going to go hell-for-leather to try to match their times or gamble on a push at the finish. I hoped we'd gamble.

Early on, the pace was slow and I got a little jumpy. After half a lap I was well boxed in and when I went to make a little move I tripped, stumbled a little and instinctively grabbed for the girl in front of me, a French runner called Zhora Kallou, to prevent myself falling. Her race number came away in my hand. Oops!

We all recovered and no harm was done, but that moment and surviving it was the difference between being here tonight for an Olympic final and being a footnote. How many moments of bad luck have other runners had in the course of not getting here, not being in Barcelona at all? Little strains. Trips and falls. Bad form. Rows with trainers.

I ran against Mary Decker Slaney in New York in the spring, and beat her. She was close to the qualifying time and I expected to see her here. Yet she didn't make it – but a girl who has been shot at by snipers in Sarajevo is here; a kid who keeps getting pneumonia or bitten by dogs is here; the best female runner in Papua New Guinea is here; a girl from Myanmar is here. I'm here. You never know when you will have your chance.

Lollipops. Christmas parties. Little things like that were the incentives which drew me in. Trips. The fun of it. We'd travel to Dublin on the train for races in Santry or Belfield. When the ticket collector came around, a gang of us would hide in the loo, leaving maybe two of our accomplices with the three tickets we had bought between us.

'The other girl is in the loo,' they would say, as sweet as pie, as the rest of us stood, shoehorned together, in the airless toilet waiting for the signal for us to come back out.

It was all small stuff but good. I remember winning the Munster Schools Under-14 title in Dungarvan and getting my picture in the paper the next week. Glory! Pat O'Halloran, a long jumper in the club, would take us to athletics meets around Munster. We loved those expeditions. It was a tradition on the way home to stop at Mandy's on the corner of Patrick Street in Cork. We'd have fishburgers because we were healthy young athletes. Fish-burgers and chips, please.

Here in Barcelona, the Olympic village has little compounds for the athletes, little rooms that aren't air conditioned: bright, freshly painted white walls reflecting the bright sunshine, without curtains to keep the light out. Kim McDonald, my manager, has booked this hotel, though. The hotel is brand new and gleaming and it sits just outside the gates of the village. There is no restaurant in the place yet (it is that new and that unfinished), but it has blinds and shutters which come down with a gentle whirr when you press a button. Another button sets off the welcome hum of the air conditioning. And if you close your eyes that is all you can hear. The roiling chaos of the village is a million miles away.

The village is so light and bright and loud and hot. But Kim has this haven fixed up for his people, and whoever has a race looming can go into the hotel for a night or two and have total peace and luxury right there, right outside the gates of the Olympic village.

The millionaire professionals of the US basketball Dream Team are staying away from the village, and everybody thinks this is bad form. So our hotel is a discreet bonus, our secret luxury. We aren't supposed to tell anybody what Kim has provided. That is just the sort of thing that Kim can do.

Gerard Hartmann, the physio and masseur, calls into the hotel to give massage treatments to those of us who need them. My friends Frank O'Mara and Marcus O'Sullivan have also stayed in the hotel while the others have baked in the village. A picture was taken the other night of the gang of us, Marcus, Frank, Gerard and myself, out in Barcelona. Our time.

All those wet days, all those evenings running in sodden fields after school, the stifling colds or bouts of flu so I would be allowed out just to run, all the rivalries and all the sessions, all the medals thrown into boxes and all the defeats brooded over for weeks. All of that leads to here. To an Olympic final and all the little things you bring to it to make you think that you have an edge, that this is your time.

A few moments ago, just as we walked to the start line with

65,000 people in the stadium suddenly attentive towards us, I glanced up and I noticed the Olympic flame burning orange against the purple night; and it struck me for the first time – I mean really hit more than anything else – that this is the Olympics. This is the dream.

Down on the track, this can be a lonely thought to find yourself holding on to just before the start of the biggest race of your life, but the night was playing tricks. I looked away from the flame and across the great wall of faces and I locked eyes with, of all people, my father. Dad grinned at me. The whole world watching but we locked for a moment. This is the Olympics but, kid, it's only a race.

The gun cracks and we shoot off at first like mildly startled animals, jockeying for position and throwing shapes at one another. It's slow. You'd think that Olympic finals would be run at full pace and that the person who could run the quickest would dictate that pace, but we are cagey and we each have our strengths.

In the 1988 Olympic final, Mary Decker Slaney went for the slash-and-burn tactic, pushing everybody out at world record pace for the first 1000 metres. She was still in front at the halfway mark but she hadn't shaken the pack.

At 2000 metres my Villanova college mate, Vicki Huber, went past Mary Decker Slaney, then Yvonne Murray went past, then Tetyana Samolenko (who is on my shoulder now, running under her married name, Tetyana Dorovskikh). They kept pouring past Mary Decker Slaney. The medallists and the fourth- and fifth-placed girls all improved their personal best times by at least seven seconds. Mary Decker Slaney finished ninth for her troubles.

There is no way anybody is going to make the same mistake tonight.

So here in Barcelona, up on the hill they call Montjuic, Alison Wyeth goes to the front for a bit. I think nothing of it. The pace doesn't get any faster just because Alison is leading us. The big guns aren't impressed or worried. So I stay tucked in with the pack. I have certain cards in my hands. Everyone else has other cards, their strengths. We play them when we see fit.

The first move that interests us is when, coming down the back straight towards the bell for the last lap, Yvonne Murray moves to the front. I have been watching Yvonne all through. She is the European Champion and, for me tonight, the favourite. Five hundred metres left and Yvonne has to go now. She got a bronze in Seoul and she ran 8:29.02 in that final. She hasn't got a devastating kick at the finish, so Yvonne needs to go now if she is to get on the podium. When she makes her move it sets a flag waving in my head.

I've been waiting for this. Yvonne plays her card and I raise her. I skip away from the pack and fasten myself on to Yvonne's frail shoulders. See ya, suckers.

And suddenly, very quickly, I realize that Yvonne's cards are all on the table and that she has been holding nothing. She goes. I go. And I realize with over 300 left that she is dead. Running on empty. The two of us aren't leaving the field behind. I am practically bumping into Yvonne's shoulder blades.

Nerves get to her, I think. Yvonne put the pedal to the floor before she was supposed to. I accelerated, just to stay with her. Now she is out of fuel. With 300 metres to go she has all but stopped. She has nothing left, and suddenly I find myself in the lead, not knowing what to do. Another fine mess!

I don't have the confidence to be out here. I just run as hard as I can, but deep down I know that I am running scared. Waiting for the worst.

We had been coming on to the start of the back straight of the final lap when Yvonne evaporated into the night and left me alone, out in front of an Olympic field and about 150 metres away from my comfort zone. It is too soon, but it is too exciting also. The crowd are clapping in rhythm, trying to urge somebody to make a move. So I go with it. I make a push. Maybe I have enough. Maybe fear and adrenalin and innocence will push me home.

Now the walls are making so much noise. All around me this massive bowl is coming alive, people are on their feet, flashbulbs are popping, the hot lava excitement has just spilled over and down on to the red oval where we have been playing cat and mouse.

I go for it. Flat out. Push. Push. Push. Down around the last bend. Legs stretching as far as they can go, arms pumping. I can't hear the footfalls behind me. I can't glance up at the immense screen. I can't see the posse, but I can tell from the noise washing over us that I am not escaping them on this last bend. They are reeling me in.

We come around on to the final straight and we are beyond thought and tactics now. Our guts are busting, our hearts are pumping. I can feel their breaths on my shoulders. One hundred metres to an Olympic medal. Ninety metres. Just down that track. I can see glory . . . No!

It's all over. I was out in front, still running, but in reality a dead girl walking. Out in front, with the world watching, and just asking questions. Why am I here? What am I doing? I couldn't handle the answers. I'd run a young athlete's race. The whole Olympics experience overtook me when I had planned it the other way around. I was racing against virtually the same people on the same size track as I always did, but next thing I knew I was getting passed. A sucker's race.

I knew it would come but still I wasn't ready for it. When they come from behind they have it all. They can see how you are going. They can make all the judgements. I got passed and they disappeared. If I had run for a medal or held my head 200, 300 metres back I would have had a chance, but I went for it. I went crazy, gambled and lost. When they pass you like this you are dead. Really just dead.

So Romanova steams past on my right. A dark blur. Eighty-five metres now to an Olympic silver I know I won't get. I hardly have time to think or react when Dorovskikh goes through on my left. They go almost in unison, reacting to each other. I know without needing to look that I don't exist for them any more.

My legs have no more power. Angela Chalmers in her red-and-blue Canadian outfit goes past me on the right, and suddenly in the space of 20 metres my story has changed. Gold. Silver. Bronze. Fourth. Footnote. The loneliest corner at the party.

There is a picture of that moment when I died. People used to come up to me and ask me to sign it. Romanova and Dorovskikh and Chalmers have all gone past and my face is just like that painting, *The Scream* by Edvard Munch. I look like I am crying but I am just screaming. I'd just watched my death.

Afterwards my dad cries. I cry. A lot of tears get spilled, but hey, hey, hey, this is a journey. It's ongoing. I have travelled. Five years ago I was a seventeen-year-old kid with a big mop of hair and I surprised everyone, myself included, by galloping away with the senior Irish cross-country title at a race in Killenaule.

The TV people were there and they asked me, 'What now?' I stood there in my black-and-yellow Ballymore-Cobh singlet and I probably should have said, 'Now? A fishburger and chips in Mandy's, please.' Or, 'Now? I'm going to do my maths homework.'

But I said, 'I'd like to run in the Olympics but sure I'll take each day as it comes.'

Now I am under the stand in Montjuic. I have run in the Olympics. It's over. Fourth place leaves you with nothing to hang round your neck, but I have run in the Olympics and I know that it was not enough. Now I have to do the second part. Continue the journey. I have to take each day as it comes. Fourth place. I run out into the night with Kim, warming down as we jog back towards the Olympic village.

I hardly know this man, but Kim listens and I talk. I unravel. I tell him I screwed up. I tell him that I got it wrong. I tell him I was so close. This close.

He tells me that I just got into the wrong place at the wrong time. He tells me that I am 22. He tells me that in my career the starter's pistol just sounded. Journey. Journey. Journey.

He lets me know that fourth is enough for today. Fourth place lets me reach my arm into the big box and pull out a lollipop. I have a career now and it's on the track. One day at a time.

2

Barcelona inspired me to be better. I needed that push. Barcelona elevated me, and I needed that too. A running career is seldom just a smooth series of laps, where you keep getting older and keep getting better until you reach a peak and then the process repeats itself except with you still getting older but slower. There are little jumping-off points all along the way.

1992 was a big year and marked the passing from one stage of my life to another. In 1992 at Le Mans, France, I got appearance money for running in a cross-country race. They paid me to be there! I got some francs; I'm not sure how much it was but it wasn't a lot, about 2,000 French francs, I think. I got a train back to Paris with a backpack on my back and a big shiny cup in my hand, and I wandered around on my own, looking for a place to have a celebratory baguette. Before that, the most I had ever received to go somewhere was £50 or £100 in expenses. This was a new world! I went there and won the race, and I got prize money on top.

I decided somewhere along the way that I believed in myself.

I hadn't won a medal in Barcelona, so I didn't come home to Cobh till September. I had work that I wanted to do and so I went on the road.

I was on a high. I broke five Irish records in ten days. I beat Romanova. Dorovskikh. Chalmers. Picked them all off like an assassin. I beat everyone who had finished in front of me in Barcelona, and when I had done that I felt happy about the idea of coming home.

That was another rite of passage. We came into the town, this place where I grew up, the daughter of the local goalkeeper, the strange girl who liked to run everywhere, and there was a big stage set up for me in the square. I have these pictures of myself standing on the stage, wearing a little skirt and my Irish top, and I can remember what was running through my head. I was thinking, this is great, everyone is saying lovely things, but what do I do? What am I supposed to do?

I went on some TV shows. I wasn't comfortable but I was prepared to give it a try. I went to the 'Sports Star of the Year' Awards. All new stuff and slightly stressful. I used to get a bit worried then, more than I would now, about being out and about. I'm a bit shy and quiet, but those things took me right out of my comfort zone. Having to get dressed up and wear proper shoes and everyone commenting about what you wear. I had no idea about fashion. I was the girl who pretended she wasn't allowed to go to discos. I had almost never been out except in a tracksuit.

It was all strange and new and it was all surprising because there were plenty of times on the road to Barcelona when I swerved off course or just took the wrong turning.

For two of my four years in Villanova I had been permanently injured and I had lost sight of what I had set out to do. Back in 1987, I had actually run a time for the 3000 metres (9:01) that would have qualified me for the Olympics in 1988 (back then you had to run the qualifying time in the actual year of the Games) but when I went to America I found I couldn't get anywhere near the time again. Suddenly I was hopeless. I stayed that way for quite a while.

Still, for all its turbulence, America made me into a real athlete. The experience grew me up fast. I loved the place the first time I saw it, just got seduced by the whole experience. It was 1987 and I'd never been to America before in my life. Cobh was my oyster. Running was just a career option.

It was Easter 1987 when I went over first. Villanova flew me across to have a look around their campus and to meet their coach and team. Back in February I had caused a bit of a surprise when I'd won the Irish Senior Cross-Country Championship, just two weeks after winning the national junior title. The traditional next step for decent Irish runners of that age is to get a scholarship to an American university.

Various colleges showed some interest in me, but Villanova were the most keen; so my first journey to America was a recruiting trip to the college whose history was closely intertwined with that great tradition of Irish middle-distance running from Ronnie Delany onwards.

Villanova would fly me out and they would hope to entice me. They liked my times and said I had potential, and they said most politely that they hoped I'd like their college and their tradition. Two girls from Villanova, Colleen Gallagher and Cassie Bradley, came to pick me up at JFK.

I came through customs rail-thin and saucer-eyed. I don't know what they were expecting me to be like, but Villanova had chosen their two chaperones well. Cassie and Colleen seemed to know straight off that I liked a little mischief. Colleen actually looked so like me that people had trouble telling us apart from the start. The idea was to whisk the new recruit straight to Philadelphia and out on to the green fields of Villanova, where I would feel reassured and at home, and maybe find some fields with cows in them to run around with.

But Cassie and Colleen saw that there was another side to me. We came in from the airport through Queens and hit the mid-town tunnel and into Manhattan for the evening.

'Get out and look up there, girl.'

I got out and looked up at the great concrete-and-glass walls of Manhattan. The evening air was warm and the noise and the smells and the taste of the city filled my senses. So this was the next stop westwards from Cobh. I loved it.

Cassie would improvise a parking spot by the sidewalk in some hectic chasm and they would let me step out into the evening air and gaze up at the walls of concrete all around me.

Up Fifth Avenue we went. Down Broadway and through Times Square. Wrong way along another avenue, followed by a crazy U-turn hung in the middle of a New York street. Every car horn in Manhattan was blasting us out of it. We three girls sat in the car giggling our heads off.

We had pizza. New York pizza. When the hot peppers came I poured them on top like salt and pepper.

'Hey, girl, you don't know what you're doing with those peppers.'

But I ate them anyway without blinking. Too proud and too competitive to give anything away. I had to prove that I was at home here as well.

When we got to Villanova I had forty-eight hours to look around and absorb it but, as Renée Zellweger said to Tom Cruise, 'They had me at hello.'

They thought the Irish connection was a big selling point, but I didn't grow up knowing all about Ronnie Delany – and to be honest I hardly knew anything about Eamonn Coghlan either. I was more into watching Liverpool as I grew up. For some reason, that was my team. I had a Liverpool school bag and a poster in the room. If Kenny Dalglish and the gang had gone to Villanova I might have been even more interested.

Everything else impressed me, though. From the buildings to the geography to the people. That was the weekend that I first met Marcus O'Sullivan. He had just won the World Indoors, so he was a bit of a hero to me. And he was from Cork. And he had a nice surname. I was actually more nervous about meeting him than I was about stepping out into the streets of Manhattan; but he was very relaxed and funny, and it was Marcus who showed me around the Villanova campus.

Marcus was able to answer lots of the questions I had about going to Villanova, and a great friendship started that weekend. It was a great novelty and a bit of a calling card for me that Marcus and I shared the same surname. Everyone thought we were related and that misconception has raised its head lots of times in the years since. It's a barometer of how the two of us look. As I got older I went from being mistaken for Marcus's sister to people assuming I was his wife, then (maybe Marcus is ageing more drastically) I went back to being his sister again.

It makes us laugh and it's sort of fitting anyway. Marcus has always been like family to me. Through good times and bad he has always cared a lot about me, even though I know there were times when I did things that made him wonder what I could possibly be thinking or what planet I was operating from.

The rush of adrenalin from the Villanova trip didn't subside till a week after I was back home in Cobh. Other colleges, Arkansas, Providence, Alabama and Arizona, had been in with a shout when it came to recruitment. After that weekend, it was a done deal in my head. A no-brainer, the Americans said.

(Funny, but it was later in 1987 at the Europa Cup in Portugal that I met Marcus again. He was with Frank O'Mara and the three of us hit it off famously. Throughout my career they were both always great for a chat and a laugh to pass the hours between meals, training and waiting for the race. At that stage in Portugal I had more or less decided to go to Villanova, but Frank was trying to put in a late bid on behalf of Arkansas, where he had gone to college. There was a lot of weighing up of Frank's 'good' list and 'bad' list for each college. I always remember Frank in his last desperate effort to sell Arkansas to me telling me that it was so chilly in Villanova that the water was so cold it froze like an icicle as it came out of the tap whenever you brushed your teeth. It was so ridiculous it was funny, and it ended all the comparisons between colleges. A typical Frank moment, though!)

There was a tradition at the time for a lot of Irish athletes to make for Providence. In part, too, that is what made me opt for Villanova. They had no tradition of Irish women going there, and if I was going to head to America I wanted the entire experience, not to create a home from home for myself, surrounding myself with Irish people and measuring myself off them all the while. I wanted to strike out on my own and measure myself against the Americans.

So Villanova it was. I came home to Ireland and got myself ready to depart to the brave new world.

As the journey goes, it was a big step. When I started running as a kid in Cobh, always late for school, always running that half-mile, I had no idea there would be anything to keep me running. I loved the sensation of it and moving fast, but early on there wasn't much glory and it was just something I liked to do.

Cobh is an island, compact and hilly; and, looking back, it seems made for running on. Early on, when I was still enamoured by camogie and basketball, I ran a few races as a sprinter. I came in watching the back of everybody else. I didn't think it would be for me, this running races lark.

Back then in Cobh there used to be an annual run round the island that we called the Milk Run. (We called it the Milk Run because, well, when you got to the other side of the island you got some free milk. They'd have churns of it back there and you'd get a big glass ladled out of the churn, and on you would go to finish the race.) One day I was entered into the Milk Run and was lolloping along with milk sloshing away inside me when a man looked at me approaching and said to me, 'You'd probably be pretty good at cross-country running.'

'And what's that?' I said, genuinely thinking that he meant running from one side of the country to the other.

He told me and I liked the idea. So at 13 I ran a cross-country race in Midleton. I really struggled but I loved it. I fell in love with the sensation of running on grass. I won my first ever cross-country race, in bare feet, and managed to take a wrong turn along the way; but I was East Cork champion that year. I knew now what I wanted.

I'd heard stories around the place about this local coach, Sean Kennedy, and the sessions he would put people through on the hills up behind the reservoir. He sounded like my kind of guy. I called him up.

So it started with Sean. He would write out a couple of weeks' worth of training routines for me. He would photocopy it and, if I saw him, he would hand the papers to me; if I didn't, he would slip them through the letterbox on his way to work.

Sean worked all hours on the shift down in Cara Partners in Little Island. I never knew what he did until Cara sponsored a race which I won and they gave me a slide projector as the prize. I sold it for £100.

Sean loved the science of running. He devoured books on the subject, especially those by Peter Coe, Seb's dad, who had coached his son all the way up to Olympic gold.

Sean went through just about every session that Seb had ever done. I received the processed and refined versions. I kept a training log at home, filling it in faithfully every night. If the times seemed impressive it was because I was guessing. Standing in a field in Cobh, I had no idea how far 100 metres was, so I settled on a satisfactory landmark and raced to that. Anything longer I just added on appropriately.

I needed encouragement, and Sean believed in my potential. He was always telling me I was destined for great things. He'd sit in our kitchen or I'd sit in his car and we'd go through sessions. I always wanted more and tougher, and sometimes he would allow me more and sometimes he would rein me in. There were times when Sean would find me inexplicably tired from sessions he had given me and I would admit, under questioning, that I had done the sessions up a hill to make them more challenging.

One day I announced to him impatiently that I wanted to be the best in the world. He told me that I had the potential if that was what I really wanted.

Running soaked into my being until it was a part of me. I would run home in the dark from anywhere I might be because I felt safer. I'd disguise colds and even flu within the house in case I would be prevented from going out for a run. We got jobs potato picking each summer, and everyone would stop to rest while the tractor went off to gather spuds from others. I'd take the chance to do a few laps of the field while they all shook their heads.

That was home: the eldest of three, good at maths and headed towards accountancy perhaps. Nothing very remarkable except an inability to stop running. A small-town girl with long strides and a head full of ambitions.

I got ready to leave. Sean sat me down and explained that Marty Stern in Villanova would be my coach from now on. I'd understood that without ever thinking about it too much. Now it was reality.

3

My stateside career started with a bit of a whimper, to be honest. In 1987 I was running in the European Juniors when I picked up my first decent injury. So I went to Villanova in the autumn with a stress fracture, a cast on my right shin and a pair of crutches on my arms.

However disappointing that was for Villanova, what happened next was a bit alarming for me. They made me take the cast off. It was a sign of things to come for me. In the next couple of years I would experience stress fractures of the left shin, the left foot and the upper left and right thigh, and myself and Villanova would lock horns again and again over how to get the best out of me.

I wondered for a while if I'd ever be OK again. I kept getting stress fracture after stress fracture, to the point where I could diagnose them without going to the physio or Blue Cross and just give myself another six weeks in the swimming pool.

During one of my prolonged periods of injury the Villanova head coach, 'Uncle' Marty Stern, wrote to my parents back in Cobh, predicting great things for me and reminding them that Eamonn Coghlan had struggled until his junior year in Villanova.

Marty told my mother and father that he was a patient man. By that time I would say he was running out of patience though.

Marty was an old-style, enthusiastic, high-octane coach who used to sell running shoes at a store called Uncle Marty's Shoe Barn in Doylestown, Pennsylvania. He had a little bit of a connection with the Ronnie Delany era. When Marty was a kid he used to go to the famous Penn Relays at Franklin Field and watch the great Villanova teams trained by Jumbo Elliott.

All the Irish business guys in Philly would come along on the Friday of the relays and sit in their hats and coats in the south stand of Franklin Field with Jumbo and wait till the distance medley was run and would then vanish. Marty would sit nearby getting little riffs of the chatter. And when he got older and got to be head coach at Villanova, that's where he would sit when we went in the Penn Relays. In the shadow and cold of the south stand. For tradition.

So Marty was old school and not hugely entertained when I blamed the running on roads and hard tracks for my injuries. Once I got this idea into my head, Marty and myself began butting heads. I wasn't happy and there were several times when I gave serious thought to just coming home for good and getting a job.

I was never really homesick, but I always found when I came home that I didn't know quite what was going on around the place. The first summer when I came home I was disillusioned with running and had been through too much with the injuries to care very much about going back.

I stayed in Villanova till just before the 1992 Olympics, but for my first two years there I was in limbo. I could tell myself that I had once been this good and now I was not that good, and I worried about how I would get myself back up there. The people I came across, the girls on the team and the assistant coaches, were always very helpful and encouraging about doing what would work.

This was the pre-Internet age. To call home on the phone back then, you went out of your way to make an arrangement and set up a time. I became a bit removed from home at that stage but I sort of looked forward to the challenge of striking out on my own. Dad would call from work at 7 a.m. My room-mate knew if the phone went in the early hours, it was my father. I became more distant, more independent. A bit more bloody-minded. I like to do things myself. It was easier for me and for everyone around me when the running got good again and I was able to do my own thing.

In the bad years my dad, on behalf of himself and Mam, made a big effort to stay in touch and find out what was going on. He spoke to Marty Stern a few times and Dad was on top of things. He knew I was a good runner and that I loved it. When I went to America, injured, and then stayed injured, he was worried.

What was I doing, he would ask. Why wasn't I improving? I would come back home and fly into Shannon and he'd come down to Shannon to meet me at seven in the morning. I came home the first time and I had gained weight, my hair was funny colours. I must have looked older, less like his daughter and less like an athlete. My mother always worried in more pragmatic ways. How would I get a job after all this?

In fairness, Villanova always encouraged me. They used to take me everywhere with them. They never wanted to leave me at home alone, even when I was injured. So when I wasn't running they would take me to big championships and meets. It was good and it made me want to be part of it. Marty Stern would say, 'Sonia, you will be back and you will run and you will win. We just wanted you to see what it is like.'

The first year I was home, I got involved for a short while in trying to misspend my youth. I'd got a job in a pub at home in Cobh, a place called the Rob Roy. Two brothers ran the place. The floor of the pub was just bare tiles, but they'd cover it in sawdust. I'd never been in there before I got a job with them. I started work for £3 an hour. I'd work from seven to twelve.

I wasn't exactly a barfly but it wasn't exactly the diet of champions either. After work we'd go to the disco in the Commodore Hotel. I think my mother thought I had gone mad. I can't drink at all, even then in the few months that made up my 'wild times'. I could hardly drink, but my mother used to tell me I was drinking too much.

Just how bad was the drink problem? There was another pub in Cobh called the Donkey. We'd go in there. I used to drink Guinness. There'd be crowds in the pub, milling at the bar, and my friends would be saying, 'Drink something else – we can't wait for that.' I wasn't committed to the Guinness. I'd drink whatever was handiest for them. My friends discovered that buying a pint

22

of Heineken was cheaper than buying the equivalent volume in two glasses. We'd get a pint and split it into two glasses. And that was us.

Still, I'd come home from America with different-coloured hair. I was going through this whole summer, working from seven to twelve and staying out really late. I always smelled of smoke and my throat would be sore in the morning. I'd get up late and go for a six-mile run every day. I'd sit around and watch *Home and Away* on telly and then leave the house at 6.55 and run down the road to get in to work on time. I didn't seem any closer to being the accountant Mam had hoped I would be.

I was sitting in the pub one night when I got talking to a local character, a man by the name of Coochie Ireland. These days Coochie is better known as the father of Stephen Ireland, the (occasional) international footballer. In his day Coochie himself was a good football player for Springfield, one of the local Cobh teams. Coochie got beaten up, down town, and he was recovering. He was not allowed drink during this time. He was bored.

He said, 'There's no way you can win that road race.'

I said, 'And why not?'

'I don't think so,' he said. 'Sure, aren't you in here every night drinking pints!'

It was the challenge I needed to make sure I won that race.

The race we were discussing was to take place in Killarney. It was advertised around the pubs and hotels. For some corny reason it was called 'The Human Race'. The first prize was a return Aer Lingus ticket to America. There was so much emigration out of Ireland at the time that an airline ticket to the USA was a pretty big deal.

So he got me thinking. It was the challenge I needed to make sure I won the race. I had to pay my air fare to get back to Villanova. If I won a free flight I'd have more money to spend on pints of Heineken and hair dye.

I decided to train for this race. This was 1989 and I hadn't run properly in quite a while. I ran 40 minutes every day for a while as usual, but when the race got closer I called my old coach Sean

Kennedy and told him of my plan. We went to the track, did a load of 600s and 400s. I don't know what sort of shape I was in but I know that I couldn't do them today.

Anyway, come the great day in Killarney I ran 15:40, a course record. At the time, to run under 16 minutes for 5 kilometres was huge. I got myself an airline ticket and I got a new interest in running. If I can do this off a few weeks' work with Sean, I said to myself, maybe I really have potential after all.

I went back to America full of confidence. I'm this good! Again! Marty Stern was excited. I was excited. I brought with me some of the training which Sean had recommended to me. *Fartleks* to be precise.

Fartleks (the word translates as speed play) are a quare name but great stuff. *Fartlek* training was invented back in the 1930s by a Swedish coach called Gösta Holmér, and it has been adopted by many coaches, physiologists, athletes and teams since. *Fartleks* were designed originally to give a bit of a boost to the poor downtrodden Swedish cross-country team, which kept getting thrashed by Paavo Nurmi and the Flying Finns.

Holmér's idea was to use a faster-than-race pace in training and to concentrate on both speed and endurance training at the same time. I started doing these sessions on the grass in Villanova.

It was a simple approach. When I had spoken to Sean Kennedy I'd said that I was running badly. He asked what I was doing in Villanova, and he just told me to go and run in the fields like I used to. I did, and it turned out to be a wise and brilliant solution.

I was still injured, starting back in 1989, so I'd go to the pool in the morning and do a session and then a little running in the evening. Basically two sessions a day. I could do the really hard stuff in the swimming pool without risk of stress fractures anyway. The more of that I did, the better I would be, I told myself.

It was all about time. At college, some athletes decided that they would hedge their bets and maybe put more time into the academic side of things and fit running in as best they could. I didn't neglect study but I put the emphasis now on my running career as much as I could. I stayed in the pool every day till my fingers were wrinkled and I had to be pulled out of the water.

By Christmas I was ready for the real thing. I took charge of myself to see what I could do. I showed Sean's proposed training session schedules to Marty Stern and he told me he wouldn't prescribe them for a horse, but that he was willing to let me try. We had a good chat. Things hadn't been great between us, but my old friend Colleen Gallagher was the mediator and Marty agreed that it was worth anything for me to have a decent shot at salvaging my college career.

The sessions I wanted to do were real gutbusters. I might start a session with 5 x 1000 metres flat out and work down through the distances from there.

Around this time too, Ronnie Delany paid a visit to the Villanova campus. I am great friends with Ronnie now but I suppose I had a wary relationship with him back then when we first met. He gave me great encouragement, while telling me that if I could get a clear run without injury I would be great.

When I finally went out training alone in America, it was strange. I remember that January, and it was freezing. The rest of the team were all inside, working out on the indoor track. I was out, running on the white fields with the snow and ice crunching under my feet.

To do that, to get out there alone and in the cold, I had to picture things in my own mind. I had to make myself believe that I would win. I would train with certain teammates and rivals in mind. During the last reps of a session I was imagining I was always beating them. All the big meets Villanova had brought me to I played little looping tapes of in my head, each one showing the last lap of a big race and myself busting a gut, racing against imaginary people with familiar faces.

It worked. I threw everything into the pot and it worked for me. Using Sean's training, I went from being injured to being third in the NCAAs in America in 12 weeks. I saw the difference. Marty Stern saw the difference. Other girls on the team saw the difference.

There was one girl on the team who was something of a legend to us. Vicki Huber had run in the 1988 Olympics while she was still a student at Villanova. (The Seoul Games were on in the autumn of that year, during the college term, and I remember lots of us getting together to watch Vicki – a person at the Olympics that we all actually knew! She came in sixth in the 3000 metres, and it was a big deal for us all.) Vicki came back to college after a year off, and a year later she was running in the cross-country season for Villanova. I was on the team with her.

All the great tradition that Villanova had on the track was tradition on the men's side of the fence. That season of 1989–90 was the first year that Villanova was lined up to win the women's team title. We had a really strong team that year.

Marty told me at one stage that Vicki came in the office and said she was really worried about me. I was too close to her in training sessions. I was keeping up. Music to my ears.

We ran in the NCAA championships. I ran poorly, with another stress fracture, but because it was the NCAAs I knew I had to run. I was the third scorer on the team, 25th or something like that. I got through it. We won.

Afterwards Marty told me that Vicki was frightened of me. She finished and went on to run international races outside of college; and after that I started to win national titles for Villanova and I came to be the best on the team. I had virtually no progression into it. All of a sudden, from hardly being on the team at all I went to being the best on the team, the one they depended on. I knew I could do it before it happened though, and I just had to get myself to do it again.

I loved Villanova. You could walk everywhere. From the track through the Jake Nevin Field House to the gym and down to the indoor track. The track was mainly for basketball players, though. In 1985 the college had won the NCAA basketball championship and still wasn't over the excitement of it. It was a huge deal.

For us, a huge deal was the NCAAs or the Penn Relays, and once Villanova broke through we had a great run in those events. We had great teams and good friendships, and that made the training and the working easier.

And we had some great days. I remember once in 1991, just before the anchor leg of the women's distance medley relay at the Penn Relays, myself and this girl Jasmin Jones of Tennessee eyeing each other. The relays are such a passionate event and there is so much pride on the line it was going to be a case of which of us cracked, me or Jasmin Jones.

The race started with a 1200-metre leg. We led at the finish of that. Next a 400-metre leg. We led at the end of that. Then Cheri Goddard took it out for the 800-metre leg, and towards the end Cheri got passed and I started the final leg, the 1600 metres, in third place. Georgetown were 12 metres ahead of Tennessee and I was starting about two metres back from Jasmin Jones.

Georgetown faded quickly. After the first of her four laps it was me in the lead with Jasmin Jones sitting on my shoulder. She would have felt that I had the strength but she had the speed. She sat and waited. With 500 metres remaining I started pulling away. Jasmin Jones faded badly. When it came to the wire she had nothing left.

We won the race with a winning time of 10 minutes 55.98 seconds, which was ordinary enough; but it was my battle with Jasmin Jones that mattered to me on the anchor leg. It was me or Jasmin Jones who would crack. I won in the end with 60 metres to spare. Maybe my best day in a Villanova singlet.

I ran my 1600 metres in 4:27.5, the fastest time ever at the Penn Relays. The time was more than two seconds better than the previous record, which had been set by Vicki Huber in 1988. It was five months after that performance that Vicki had run in the Olympic 3000-metre final in Seoul.

When you ran for Villanova you scored for the team, and that closeness and those friendships made for good times. We used to get packed into a van and driven to nearby Haverford College for some indoor training in the winter, and Haverford would train on our outdoor track come the spring. Over there in Haverford I was close to Marcus and to his coach, Tom Donnelly, who used to be the coach there.

Those trips to Haverford in the van were always a giggle, the gang of us thrown together like a proper team. When we arrived, the girls would train indoors. I would run outside on the Haverford Trail, alone with my thoughts. I got to love that part of the world and I ended up living there after I graduated from Villanova.

Other parts of my life also fell into place in Villanova. I had had no boyfriends for two years in America, and then Terrence Mahon transferred into Villanova from Oregon. He would be my only boyfriend in America.

We became quite friendly and close. Terrence was big into nutrition and made a ritual of going to the market to get fresh fruit and veg every day. We all stayed in dorms in the college and ate what we were served up with in the dining hall, but Terrence taught me a lot about food and health and well-being. He was a fine runner and I used to run a lot with him. Those last couple of years in Villanova, great years for the Wildcats (as we were known), had a big influence on me. I started to get really fit and I came to understand that being fit wasn't just a matter of being able to run faster than people the same age as myself. I became obsessed with writing down training routines in some detail.

Villanova ended my girlhood days just before Barcelona ushered me into the next chapter of my life, a perfect baton pass.

4

Between college and Barcelona I had dabbled a little in the big bad world of professional athletics; but I stepped out on to the circuit with a bit more confidence after the Olympics. Missing out on a medal by 0.19 of a second was something you could take in one of two ways. It was tragedy or it was something hopeful. If you are young and 0.19 of a second separates you from being a success, the feeling of tragedy is temporary.

In 1992, when I started to get better results on the track, I began to feel as if I belonged in the great athletics circus. I had my own rivals and targets and my own agenda. That made a difference. I had progressed as an athlete in the final two years of my time in Villanova but probably not as much as I should have overall during those four years of my career.

Before the Games I had sampled this world in little cautious tastings. I had run the World Student Games in Sheffield in 1991, and back in 1990 I had run in the European Championships, but I hadn't been in any really big races except Europa Cup and Irish team stuff.

(Sheffield was special and it was also the first time I ever came across the Chinese. I ran the 3000 metres. There were no heats, just a huge race. I was supposed to win but I came in second. In the 1500 metres, in the heats a Chinese girl went out and ran 4:07 and finished miles ahead of everyone. That was Qu Junxia. I have a picture of her at home. I won the final in a blanket finish. 4:12. Six of us in there, and she was second. In 1992 she was third in the 1500 at the Olympics but nobody would have paid any attention. I was fourth in the 3000. I was the only one taking any notice of a Chinese presence in Barcelona. I was saying to myself that I had beaten her last year!)

There is a difference between the college and the team environment and getting out there on your own and racing for a living. You have to earn your right to feel as if you belong out there.

In 1991 I had run in Crystal Palace for the first time. I had to call up Andy Norman, who practically ran UK athletics at that time, and ask if I could run. I had just run an Irish record of 15:26 over 5000 metres at the Irish Championships in front of about five people at the CIT track in Cork; I thought I was pretty hot stuff and that everyone would want me. I was doing him the favour, I reckoned. He wasn't too impressed but he let me in.

The reality is never like you imagine it. Crystal Palace! I had seen Crystal Palace on television so many times. They used to feature men's races a lot more on TV back then. Cram and Ovett and the boys. I had this vision of Crystal Palace as some sort of gleaming pleasure dome. It wasn't.

I'm not sure how I got there, but I remember we stayed in Croydon at the Croydon Park Hotel. One of my Villanova friends, Gina Procaccio, was going to be there from America. Gina was getting $1,000 to race. I was having trouble wangling two tickets for my Auntie Fran to come and see me, but the prospect of company was all I focused on. Knowing somebody, that was a big thing, going to these early races. Not knowing anyone. Who would I talk to? It was like starting a new job. Would I go into the athletes' eating area alone? Would I go to the warm-up area on my own?

I had to know somebody, had to have somebody to cling on to. In later years I would go into the athletes' eating area and nobody would dare to come and sit next to me, they'd leave me alone. Back then though, I had to pay my dues.

So I shared a room with Gina Procaccio and was thrilled with myself. That was a tough thing about starting out on the circuit. You had to organize room-mates for yourself. Once I ended up with a Russian shot putter who smoked. I was shocked. Some of the high jumpers would smoke too. If you couldn't organize a friend to share with, you took pot luck sharing with smoking Russians or high jumpers.

When you start on the circuit there are small things to learn. Most of the time, getting ready for a race you are outside doing your warm-ups and eyeing people up. In Crystal Palace for instance, there is a little field beside the stadium and a wire fence separating you from the arena. All the managers and coaches hang around in there. It's a place of business as well as a place of sport.

When I began going to meets by myself I was paying attention to other people all the time, looking for familiar famous faces and measuring myself against them and worrying that I would never make it. Everyone goes jogging around a small track for the warm-up. You see all the opposition. You warm up beside somebody who is flying and it gets into your brain. I remember seeing the great Mary Slaney warming up once. I couldn't keep pace with her warm-up jog. I decided I needed a system in order to deal with my rivals even during warm-up. I'd check, and once I had seen them all and knew they were all there I would try to block them out of my thoughts after that.

I changed that technique further as I went on. When I got a little more confidence I would always run the opposite way to everyone else who was warming up. If they ran clockwise, I ran counter-clockwise, so everyone else would be running in the same direction as they would run around the track proper and I always went the wrong way.

I wasn't being contrary, and obviously I would nearly run into people, but I liked being able to see the faces of the other runners.

There was also something psychological to it: it probably bothered other runners. A Boulmerka or a Szabo is coming up to you from the opposite direction, you are eyeing each other. Who is going to change lane first? Will we both go the same way to avoid a collision? It's a game of chicken.

At first, of course, I made eye contact with everyone who came past; but once I got confident about it, I realized that there was no need to be saying 'Hello' every time you passed somebody. I'd just go head down. I got to the point where I might as well have been wearing blinkers.

Blinkers. Looking back, that is what happens when you come

away from the track when it has really absorbed you. You forget to take those blinkers off. You are focused in on what you have to do next. It's like method acting: you live it. By 1993, as soon as I finished one race I wanted to know what was next, what was the next training session, what would I be doing every day the next week before the next race. I had to know what I was moving on to. Nothing really existed outside of racing.

In 1991 I had run a race in Lille. I ran a pretty bad race tactically, but I came through from the back to almost win it and was well enough pleased with myself. Afterwards Frank and Marcus were chatting to me. Their manager was there too, Kim McDonald. He wasn't shy about telling me that I had run badly, a real negative race. I thought he was cheeky and full of it, but I was challenged by him too. I liked him.

When I think about blinkers and that period of my life when I wore them all the time, Kim was there with me throughout. He became my agent, my boyfriend and my coach. Whatever obsession I may have had with running, Kim could take it and beat it with his own obsession. We shared a sort of madness when it came to running.

After Barcelona in 1992 I just ran a load of races in succession. Whatever was there, I went in for it. I ran them all. A 1500 in Monte Carlo and I beat Angela Chalmers, for instance. Put a line through her name in my head. It was like a little game. I had to beat everyone who had finished ahead of me. I had a bit of a battle with Romanova in the 3000 in Brussels. There was a bit of pushing on the top bend with 150 metres to go, but I came off better. I was learning.

In 1993 the first race I had was against Romanova in Hengelo. Jos Hermans (who is Haile Gebrselassie's manager) was organizing the race and Jos came and asked us what pace we would run. I piped up, 'Sixty-eight seconds.' Romanova said nothing. Jos said to me, 'Are you sure?'

I said, 'Yes.'

It's not just about racing, it's about making the others feel that you are unbeatable. I beat Romanova by half the length of the track that night. It was a big breakthrough. Another name crossed off.

That left a lingering rivalry with Yvonne Murray. Yvonne was pretty dominant, from 1990 when she won the Europeans right through to 1992 in the Olympic final when I watched her all the way. I was watching her. For loads of races in 1993 and 1994, maybe ten races in all, the result was exactly the same, the two of us first and second. Those rivalries eased me into the Grand Prix circuit, and before I knew it I was successful at that level.

Yvonne was quiet and she always had her coach with her. I had Frank and Marcus, two comedians. We were referred to as the Irish mafia. The boys would set up shop and all the Irish would join them. I was the kid sister, tucked safely under their wing. Being around Frank and Marcus gave me some protection and insulation.

On the circuit you see fame really close up. It takes a while to realize we are all the same anyway. I'd see Linford Christie parading about the hotel with that strut that sprinters have and just think, wow, I saw Linford Christie. He said hello to me one day and I rang my mother to tell her. I roomed with Sally Gunnell once. I just looked at her in awe. Little things like that. You feel you are seeing fame close up, and then at some point you just stop noticing. That process was accelerated listening to Frank and Marcus take the mickey out of every person and every situation.

We'd be in a lift, say, in the race hotel. Everybody keenly aware of who everybody in the lift was. Everyone staring ahead. And Frank would say in a loud voice, '*Feach ar an gruaig ar an fear seo!*' And the three of us would nod earnestly, each silently daring the others to explode with laughter.

They would have jokes going constantly, pulling people's legs all the time, making up stories. I would never know what was serious or not. There would be telephone calls from one or the other of them pretending to be journalists, asking questions that started out serious and got more and more ridiculous. They were good at it and you couldn't be sure. You wouldn't like to be insulting to a journalist, but sometimes even doing genuine phone interviews there was always a voice in your head saying, this is Frank O'Mara winding me up.

Marcus was always more sensible and he could see things clearly. You'd go to him for real advice. Frank was great fun and kept things lighter. Marcus and Gerard Hartmann would go for walks in the evening and have philosophical conversations about everything to do with athletics. They'd walk for two hours, talking about heart rates.

Gerard was the last piece of the jigsaw for me. I had known him in Barcelona. In 1993 I had a little injury and Kim suggested I go see Gerard in Florida. It was great. I'd had just a little niggle. I felt that I could still run, I went down there for a few days, and went on and won my next race.

The guys would rescue me all the time. Some disaster would be about to happen, anything from a race to training to dealing with the media. I would be about to fall apart. They would come in and save me. If things weren't working out physically I would go to Gerard. He'd sort me out. For my head I had the choice of the three of them.

They were my protectors and advisers. Sometimes I would get it into my head that I wouldn't talk to anybody. They would say, maybe you should.

On the circuit I was so glad of them. Everyone was settled into their own groups: the Russians were the Russians – the Kenyans, the Ethiopians – each had their own groups. We were all on tour, part of this circus. The African runners were very friendly but they stuck together at the tables and stuff.

You had all these cultural groups around the place. Then there were other divisions, by discipline or the way people dressed. You could tell groups that way. The sprinters always bring a whole wardrobe with them, mainly for when they are preening in the lobby. Some people only ever wear tracksuits and go around with a backpack welded to their back and running shoes always on their feet. Others always get dressed up the night after the meet.

I was in the middle of this. When we came back from the race we would go to our rooms, have an ice bath and shower and come down. It was a bit friendlier then. Nowadays people come straight from the track, in for a really quick dinner, out and gone.

We would hang around upstairs a lot and trade the gossip. There was always something going on. Some people live for the gossip. I'm never really into it, but it passed the time.

If somebody slept with somebody else the whole circuit would know before morning. Always something going on, especially among the young ones! I was protected from such things. I just wasn't allowed. My little army of chaperones.

I remember Paula Radcliffe and Gary Lough when they were first going out and there was some big deal in the hotel lobby in Monaco. Some fuss about them sharing a room or not sharing a room. Everyone knew about it. They had to find two other people who would swap. They didn't want to announce it to the world, but they had to go and look for two people to swap. It played out like a high school drama.

I was living in London and began spending time with the Kenyan athletes in Teddington, and I saw the simplicity of their lives and was influenced by that too. They weren't into shopping or tourism. I thought that was the way to go.

I was training with the Kenyans and was involved in a different group, and I started looking to other sources for advice. I grew apart from Sean Kennedy and probably didn't handle it well. I never discussed the changing situation with Sean or came and talked to him about it. For the Olympics in 1992 and afterwards he was still faxing me the fortnightly training schedules.

I went to the track one day, though, and was undecided about doing a session of 5 x 800-metre runs or one where I stepped down from 1000 metres to 600 metres to 400. I wrote a note to Kim and asked him what I should do. He said, do this. Do it in these times. He was so certain of himself that it was very persuasive.

I came home in 1993 and ran in the Cork City Sports and lost to Aisling Molloy. I had a chat with Sean after that. I was fuming. He was looking to console me. He told me that one bad race didn't make me a bad runner. I said to him that I had a different coach now.

I suppose it was inevitable, but your first serious coach is like your first serious boyfriend, they will always mean a lot to you. Sean was very nice about it all and we never had a problem. It did worry me for a while; we had been through a lot together and his encouragement and advice had brought me to the point where I was able to spread my wings and fly away.

Socially, because of my college background I always hung around with a lot of Americans. A big group of American girls stayed in Europe during the summer season and hung around with each other. I tagged on. We'd go for runs together, the shops and the zoo. All that stuff. They were good company and good friends, but at the business end they were always a bit frightened when some pace was injected into the race.

The way it worked was: when you come into the race hotel there would be an athletes section at check-in and there would be a big notice board up with sheets for competitors telling everyone where to go, how to get your number, the times of shuttle buses to the track, etc. Eventually, on the day of the race a sheet would go up saying what the time would be for the early laps and who the pacemaker or rabbit would be.

In those days it wasn't so obvious who the pacemaker in a race would be. It could be anybody back then, but after a while they started getting specialists. There is no clear-cut procedure for deciding what pace a race goes out at, but it's generally down to the leading athletes. The race organizers want a good race with the big names running fast. After I had a few successes Kim began coming to me and asking what pace did I want. I'd say I didn't know. Kim would suggest a number. I would say, OK, that's fine.

So, for a time, every time I was going out it was going to be fast pace. I like that. Organizers liked it.

Somebody has to decide; if you are the best in the race, it is up to you. The others decided whether to keep up. Most just decided not to. If the weather was bad, people would grumble. They used to come and say, you aren't going that fast, are you? I felt if you agreed to go that fast you had to try. Even if it was impossible you had to try.

For a while a girl called Maria Akraka from Sweden paced me quite a lot. Maria competed in the 1500- and 800-metre races in Barcelona and was a good athlete. We became friends and she would be happy for me to run really well. It was a strange relationship, sort of a team thing.

Rabbits would be paid separately, depending on the race. If we broke a world record or a European record they would get a bonus from the meet promoters.

Now, 10, 15 years later, it is different. It is very structured now. Back then it was more relaxed. There might be a pacemaker, and sometimes there might not.

(My old rival Jasmin Jones from the Penn Relays turned up as a pacemaker to me in Oslo in 1994. I was going for a world record in the mile. She ran the first 200 way too slow and everyone thought she did it on purpose. It was really poor. Everyone was furious. She explained it all by saying that she had been annoyed or bothered by something. I remember running into her back and saying, 'Faster, faster.' I was on her heels. 'Go faster. Go faster.' I was so fit by then and it was going too slow. I could tell the pace was way off. Sometimes I would be following the right pace and I would be saying go faster, go faster anyway. That night we were disastrously off the pace. It was a shambles. The world record was 4:16.71. I ran 4:17.25 – so close I could just about reach out and touch it, but I never got my name on that record.)

At other times the whole thing would fall apart and the pacemaker would go on and win the race. It happened once in Brussels with this girl, Yvonne Graham – actually she nearly pulled it off twice. In Brussels I was in the race and so was Hassiba Boulmerka. We were watching each other like hawks. For some reason we decided not to go with the pace. We just kept watching each other. Yvonne got further and further ahead and she went on to win.

Yvonne was a good friend of mine. I liked her and I used to ask her to act as pacemaker whenever she could. We were in Rieti one time and Yvonne had come specifically to pace the mile race. She was from Germany but was running for Jamaica. This Rieti race was a year later and the weather was so bad that even I was saying we can't really run fast tonight.

It was the end of the year and I was tired. Yvonne got ahead. With 100 metres to go, she was well clear. It was funny. Yvonne was spent. Almost running backwards. I didn't have much more. Somehow I gathered some speed and passed Yvonne right on the line. I got away with that one but lost the other one in Brussels. People love it when that happens. Yvonne and I just stood and looked at each other and laughed.

In 1993 the season started well and got better. I won everywhere and my confidence grew with it. I was aware of my strength and I knew from watching other runners that I had to project a persona. I had to give off an aura of strength. If you do that, it protects you in the races when you are feeling bad or tired.

Sometimes, when you are young, you get confused between yourself and your own persona. Once winning has become easy it becomes a form of control. Losing that control is frightening. You need to know you have everyone on the ropes. So you ignore the questions your body is asking. I won, I'd tell myself. I won, so everything is OK. End of story.

By the time summer was in full swing I was hot favourite for a gold medal in the World Championships in Stuttgart. I was probably the only person even slightly haunted by the Chinese presence at the Sheffield World Student Games. However, if I spoke about the Chinese to anybody, I would be told that the Chinese runners had made no impact in Barcelona.

OK! I was strong. I was young. I was confident. I had my persona. No impact! I could buy that. Why be afraid of ghosts?

5

I missed the Cork City Sports in 1993 to go to the Bislett Games in Oslo. It wasn't a popular decision in my home place. The organizers had arranged a rematch with Yelena Romanova as the centrepiece of the evening, but all summer I was focused on the World Championships in Stuttgart. Oslo was where I had to be.

The year 1993 would be transformative, a big step on the ladder from being a hopeful to being a contender. I went back to America in the springtime and did normal training, but when I came back to Europe I stepped it all up and my body shape changed. I lost seven or eight pounds. I got tougher and stronger.

Life now was all about training. In those first few years on the circuit from 1993 onwards, I was living in Teddington and I didn't know that nearby Kingston even existed. It seems impossible now. There was this huge big shopping venue just nearby, and I was so focused and obsessed I never knew it was there. I had a bike I would ride around a bit to save me walking everywhere. That was it so far as my travels in London went.

In another sense, though, my life was all movement. I moved from being a student athlete to becoming a full-time athlete. I moved to a different way of living when I came back from America in the autumn of 1993. For a long time I had told myself that it was impossible to run well in the mornings, and that perfect reasoning excused me from a lot of track training. Now however I started training twice a day. Track in the morning, park or the gym in the afternoon.

I was told by Kim that I should go to the track in the morning. He said that the Kenyans all went; they would go at 11 a.m., and the track would be free after that. I said, OK, I may as well just go with the Kenyans at eleven. At least the Kenyans knew what they were doing. At that time I was living in Teddington, sleeping on a pull-out bed in an apartment that Kim kept for athletes. It was near the track and the park, and that was my life.

The new regime made me a better runner and strengthened my belief that the harder I worked, the better I would become. I won seven of my first eight races that season and by the time of the Bislett Games in Oslo I was getting $4,000 for appearing in a race. Not crazy money, but better than two tickets begrudgingly coughed up at Crystal Palace for my auntie to come and watch me run.

My first big breakthrough on the European circuit had been in 1992 in Hengelo. I loved it. Elana Meyer and Margareta Keszeg had led the race away and somehow I had just kept up with them and won. I surprised myself as well as them, I think. It was a really warm Sunday afternoon, Elana's first race in Europe, and I managed to steal the show. I picked up my prize and walked away. Elana was a bit of an enigma to the sporting world, having run superfast times in South Africa, and she was now racing on the European tracks as South Africa were re-entering the sporting arena. I wouldn't have been deciding the pace at that stage so I just followed them and, hey presto, somehow I won. I was amazed. I couldn't believe I was winning races.

The following summer I was looking forward to getting back. This night in Oslo would be a memorable one. It brought Yelena Romanova (who had been bumped by the Cork City Sports when I pulled out), Yvonne Murray, Elana Meyer and myself together on a starting line again.

The Bislett Games in Oslo are a special place for athletics, a small, noisy stadium, fans who know their sport and a track that produces a lot of world records.

By the time the gun cracked the atmosphere in the old stadium was electric. The Bislett crowd make this strange noise, a bit like a train going, when a race is running well. It lifts you, chucka-chucka-chuck.

From the start I went with the pacemaker and she did such a good job that when she dropped off just before the 2000-metre mark I was surprised that Yvonne and Elana were still with me.

That's how strong I felt. So I slowed down deliberately and allowed them to get past because I could feel them clipping my heels. That's how confident I felt.

I let the girls get away for a lap and when I reached for the power in my legs it was there. I kicked with 200 to go and it was the greatest feeling, the volume of the crowd went up, I pulled away and knew that this time when I looked around there would be nobody on my heels.

I'd covered the last 400 metres in 59.8 seconds, and the best thing about it was that I finished, feeling that I had run within myself. Three weeks previously I had run a personal best of 8:33.40 in Hengelo, but tonight here in Oslo this was the run that I had been looking for as a reward for the work I had been putting in all year.

I finished in 8:28.74, a time that people are telling me is the eighth fastest ever recorded by a woman over the distance. It was a time which would have won me a gold medal at any of the previous World Championships. Just as importantly from my point of view, it is almost 12 seconds inside Romanova's gold medal winning mark from Barcelona.

In the grand plan for the year, Oslo was to be the bridge between the failure at Barcelona and the expectations for the World Championships in a few weeks. That was the plan, and it was unfolding just fine – but there was news in the week after Oslo of a faster 3000 having been run in China within twenty-four hours. But it's not on the television or on Ceefax. It's like when a tree falls in the forest and nobody sees it happen and philosophers wonder if it really took place at all. A fast 3000 metres in China? Did it really happen? The world takes place here on the Grand Prix circuit, doesn't it? We paid no heed.

Take out Stuttgart, and in 1993 I had a good year, a very good year. Everything fell into place. I stepped up into serious training. I found a place for myself on the Grand Prix circuit and a streak of good wins gave me confidence. The first race of the year was a 3000 metres against Yelena Romanova. I ran 8:31 and I had her well beaten. From then on it got better and better. Everything pointed towards success at the World Championships. I went to Stuttgart quietly confident.

The Chinese were a sensation before they even got on to the track in the Gottlieb-Daimler Stadion. For the little travelling circus of us who went from city to city in the summertime racing against each other, they were something new and strange and worrying. People would go to the track during the mornings and just watch them train. From the time the championships started, the Chinese were all we talked about. On a circuit where we were always conscious of our differences, the Chinese united us by being so different and so far removed from us.

We didn't see them in the dining room. So we talked about what they were eating. There were rumours of turtle blood; people had visions of darkened rooms and turtles being slaughtered.

The Chinese kept to themselves, but somehow they were in-escapable. When you are racing at that level you are very conscious of how what you do or say impacts on the psyches of your rivals. Whether they meant to or not, the Chinese got into all our heads. For most people they were a distraction, a novelty, but for the few of us who had hopes of medals they were more. We were the ones who would have to go out and win. And we weren't sure we could do that.

If I went to the warm-up track and ran in the opposite direction to everyone else, maybe it spooked a few rivals. When the Chinese went to the same track and ran in unison, all kitted out identically and doing everything together, it spooked everybody. People were fascinated. People were scared. Why couldn't they warm up like everybody else?

Myself, I was more scared than fascinated; but a couple of nights before the heats I had a dream that was slightly prophetic. I dreamed that I was drawn in the third heat in the 3000 metres and I arrived at the stadium to discover that the race had already started. As it happened, I did actually get drawn in the third heat, a draw that gave me a chance to see what was out there. Qu Junxia, a bronze medal winner in the 1500 metres a year ago in Barcelona, was reckoned by everyone to be the best of the Chinese at this distance. She was in heat two. The opening heat included the Olympic champion Yelena Romanova and Yvonne Murray. In my own heat was the Chinese girl, Zhang Lirong, whose career-best figure of 8:35.05 was six seconds outside my own best from Oslo.

The heats at a big championship are interesting business for competitors but not scary when you are going well. In Stuttgart, the first four in each heat plus the three fastest losers got to qualify. Life could be worse.

I won my own heat without too much of a panic. I went away from Zhang Lirong on the last lap (62 seconds, the fastest last lap in the heats) just to see what she had, and she never really responded.

There was slightly more worrying stuff in the other heats, though. A girl called Zhang Linzi, who was the World Junior Champion the previous year, seemed to have no worries at all in burning off Yvonne and Yelena in their heat. And Qu Junxia looked good in beating off a series of challenges to cross the line in 8:49.20. My own qualifying time was 8:50.62.

I was pleased, though. I had wanted to win to prove a point to others and to do it while still feeling relaxed. I felt I had succeeded in the first part and I was in no doubt at all about the second part.

So to a Monday night in the Gottlieb-Daimler Stadion in a lovely little campus in Stuttgart. It was a warm, humid evening with the temperature up into the seventies and a little foreboding in the air, but not too much. A 3000-metre final that ended in an unprecedented 1–2–3 finish for the Chinese girls, Qu Junxia, Zhang Linzi and Zhang Lirong.

Unless you are Chinese I suppose what happened was disappointing, terribly disappointing – a little bit of athletics history at which I was an innocent bystander. Looking back, it seems like a major moment; but at the time the challenge immediately afterwards was to find a way of putting the 3000 metres out of my mind and focusing fully on the races that lay ahead.

I still had the 1500 metres to look forward to. People wanted me to channel some anger at the Chinese, to point a finger, but that summer I was lying second only to the Romanian girl Violeta Beclea as the fastest 1500-metre runner in the world for the year. It wasn't all doom and gloom. There was another race to run.

Still, at times it felt like my emotions were all mixed up as I tried to work out how things could go so badly wrong in the space of eight and a half minutes. It was one of those situations in which everything you know suddenly seems to be wrong. Hard to rationalize it all. I came to Stuttgart among the favourites, if not *the* favourite, for gold. And here I was in the same old spot when the medals were being handed out at a major championship, just off stage.

Disappointment and anger all mixed up. I wasn't angry in the fingerpointing way that everyone wanted me to be. I was angry that I didn't realize that, when the Chinese girls made the break, it was going to be the decisive move. I had reckoned at that point that it was all a bit of a fake, but I got it wrong. I had never really seen the Chinese girls before, let alone seen them run, and it was hard to judge and difficult to make the right plans. When they went so early and stayed gone, they made the rest of us look foolish tactically.

They ran as a team, and in athletics that puts everyone else at a big disadvantage. The girls were talking to each other throughout the race, making space for each other when they needed it, and overall they acted a little like a basketball team. I heard afterwards that their coach, the famous Ma Junren, was in the stand encouraging them and coaching them.

We'd gone slow through the first 1000 metres, coming through behind the Romanian girl, Luminita Zaituc, at 2:59.06, but soon afterwards the pace quickened dramatically. People made their moves or pretended to. Yvonne Murray made a little burst at one stage, but memories of Barcelona were in everybody's mind. The pace quickened out of respect but nobody truly believed that Yvonne was making a serious play quite so early.

In the speculation beforehand a lot of people had assumed that the Chinese girls would go flat out, straight from the gun. We were all prepared for that on the line at the start; but it didn't happen, and perhaps we relaxed into a familiar pattern after that. Anyway, this should have been my sort of race. The field got scattered and other girls dropped off the pace one by one.

Yvonne made another burst with two laps remaining, but again we just kept her in sight and kept on watching each other. I was in fifth place at this stage behind Yvonne and then the three Chinese girls, who were running one after another in single file. Everyone holding something back, everyone waiting for something to happen. Tick. Tick. Tick.

I was still confident I could handle the situation at that point and I waited and waited. When the big move came I would be able to cover it. Of course I would.

And yet. When the move actually happened I was totally un-prepared. With about 700 metres left, I remember my friend Alison Wyeth coming on to my shoulder and being slightly distracted at that very moment as the Chinese girls suddenly picked up the pace.

Nothing more than a couple of seconds, but they were up and away before I could respond. By the time I was going they had gone: in the space of the next 200 metres they had left me. At the bell I was some 10 metres adrift of the last of the Chinese girls and the pace was such that I knew I wasn't going to catch all three of them. I set my eyes on the back of Zhang Lirong in third place. I thought I could still get third place but, but, but . . .

By the time we were in those critical last two laps we were really moving. We went through the final 800 metres in 2 minutes 3.2 seconds. In fairness, Qu Junxia, the winner, put in a great last lap of just 59.5 seconds; better still, the split showed her at 29.4 seconds for the last 200 metres. Good running.

Me? In the end I ran out of track. I came through the line and stopped there to look at the action replay being shown on the giant television screen. Apart from Qu, I had run the final 120 metres faster than anybody in the field. I'd left it too late, though. Fourth again. A disappointment with precedents. I was comfortable until the Chinese girls took control with 600 metres left. They had suddenly pulled away from the field one after the other like a train picking up steam. I was torn between going with them and calling their bluff. By the time I made up my mind, I had lost touch.

And that was it. My first 3000-metre defeat in almost a year. Another fourth place for my collection. Another big lesson learned. I'd have to grow from here. Again.

It was a short, sharp lesson. When the Chinese went, they were gone, and I had said to myself, sure, they can't be gone for good. But they were. I had only planned for the obvious. Everybody had been talking about the Chinese and it was at the back of my mind that they might do what everyone was saying and go from the gun. Beyond that I didn't have many plans. Maybe I should have looked into it more, but I didn't. That gap I left open was the end of the race for me.

I felt good physically though, and for much of the race I did everything right. I ran offensively at times, defensively when I had to do so, and I was alert to everything that was happening over the first 2000 metres. The Chinese girls had run as a team and in the end they simply shut me out.

Anger. Everyone seemed angry and wanted me to be part of it. My time of 8:33.38 was more than four seconds slower than Qu Junxia but it was even further behind my own Irish record that I had set in Oslo five weeks earlier. People were talking in headlines about the great Chinese takeaway etc., but my anger was as much at myself for getting suckered tactically. Another mistake. Another fourth place. I wasn't angry with the Chinese. I had been beaten in a time I was quite capable of running. When that happens you have to look at yourself.

I ran home with Kim and decided to treat the night in the same way as I had treated every other defeat. I decided to learn something from defeat and to come back stronger.

6

If the 3000-metre final in Stuttgart was a surprise, there were no surprises left for me the following weekend when we went to the line for the 1500-metre final. By then the Chinese looked like sweeping up all the women's track events, from 800 metres to 10,000 metres. Indeed, it was being said about the place that the 10,000-metre runner Wang Junxia could have won that range of events plus the marathon by herself if the scheduling had been more leisurely.

Questions were being asked. Not very polite questions. By the end of the World Championships, with the Chinese it had become very much a stand-off. Us and them.

For me, things were more simple. The Chinese girls in the 1500 metres were not so much a distraction for me, more a point of focus. I had to change my target. I knew that all the whispers and rumours we had ignored on the way to Stuttgart had faces and names attached to them now. This was serious. I had to at least beat one of the Chinese girls in the 1500-metre final.

So I disregarded everyone else in the race. Told myself that I just had to beat one Chinese girl and that would be enough. I regretted in the 3000 metres having let them run as a team and not tried to get in and split them. For the 1500 I was determined to pick one of them off.

Looking back now, the 1500 wasn't a race I would have been very confident in. I never thought I was that great over the distance. My style was more strength than speed, but the World Championships were in danger of turning into a humiliation for me. It was back-to-the-wall stuff.

Just before the start of the race, I looked across the stadium and saw that a medal presentation ceremony was about to begin. An Olympics and a World Championship at my peak, and I hadn't been on a podium yet. There and then, I vowed to myself that I would be up there on that stand before the end of the day.

So off we went. Watching each other like hawks. The focus in the stadium was on the Chinese, and on the track it was the same. All eyes on the girls in the white vests. Round and round, watching. Waiting. With 400 metres to go, one of the Chinese girls, Liu Dong, made the decisive break. You could almost hear the stadium tense up.

Again Ma Junren, the Chinese coach, was in the stand giving instructions. By now everyone knew his face and his voice and where he would be. During the 1500-metre final a lot of people went down there to where he was standing and blocked him off when the runners came around by jumping up and down and waving flags and trying to get in his way. Everyone in the race knew exactly where he was this time, too. His voice stands out a lot. Normally you wouldn't know or care. In the 3000 metres, when he had told them to go together with 700 to go, they had all gone together. This time the atmosphere was different.

When Liu Dong went, the response was predictable. Lu Yi, her colleague, went with her as if she was her bodyguard. Then Hassiba Boulmerka from Algeria, the surly Olympic champion, followed. Normally Boulmerka and I would be serious rivals, but in this race the Chinese were all that mattered. I followed in fourth place.

When Liu surged, she went quickly, and early on in the last lap it became clear that the rest of us were battling for the minor medals.

I felt strong and made my move from fourth position with just under 200 metres to go. Coming off the last bend, I looked up at the screen at the far end of the stadium and knew that there was a silver medal in the race for me. The gap between Liu and myself was such that I was never going to get to her, but I was convinced that I had the beating of the other two on the run-in.

So it was. Liu Dong got home in just over four minutes (4:00.50) and I came in at 4:03.48. Silver! Boulmerka behind me for the bronze and Lu Yi, the other Chinese girl, ended up in my old spot: fourth place and out of the medals. All the tension that had been building up in the stadium throughout a week of suspicion and accusation suddenly exploded. The Chinese had won gold but it hadn't been a blanket finish for the medals. The place went wild.

Poor Liu Dong did her lap of honour to near silence in the stadium. I was so excited that I did one of my own, not to milk the anti-Chinese sentiment but because I had achieved what I had set out to achieve when I redrafted my goals in Stuttgart. I had separated the Chinese and had got a medal. The triumph was personal. And I had beaten Boulmerka, the Olympic champion, into the bargain. Boulmerka, who had her own battles (being a woman from a Muslim country which constantly tried to keep her down), grinned and set off on a lap of honour of her own to celebrate third place. That was odd for a woman who had been the Olympic champion at the distance the year before, but it was that sort of night. It was like it was a victory for everybody.

Somebody gave me a stuffed toy which I clung on to. It seemed right. The monkey was off my back.

Everyone was unhappy about the Chinese that week in Stuttgart, and the silver medal was celebrated in a way as if it was one for 'us'. That was a feeling I was uncomfortable with. I wanted to engage the Chinese. On the track that night, it felt like a gold medal win. I was excited crossing the line. I was up there with them. I did the lap of the track – which is odd if you are second, I suppose – but it was one of those things that mean different things for different people. I felt that I was learning to compete with this new phenomenon.

Was I cheated by the Chinese? Yes or no? Years later, people are still asking me the question. I think I leave a lot of people frustrated that I haven't more anger about it. In an ideal world I would have won both those races in Stuttgart. When I was that young, to have won two World Championships would have changed my career. Who knows which way?

I came away with a silver from two races that I might have had gold in.

I suppose what happened in Stuttgart, while it was controversial at the time, came to be seen in an even harsher light in the weeks, months and years that followed. Stuttgart finished in August. The Chinese National Games were in September.

In the space of a few days the certainties which underpinned the athletics world as we lived it on the Grand Prix circuit were buckled still further. You can lose a race, through tactics or form or bad luck or being taken by surprise; but times and records are sacred to a runner. They are the building blocks of athletics history, they are what we measure ourselves against.

In six days, from 8 September through to 13 September, Wang Junxia, who was just 20 years old, changed everything we thought we knew about women's athletic potential. To start with, she ran the 10,000 metres in 29 minutes 31.78 seconds, to break the world record (set by Ingrid Kristiansen of Norway in 1986) by 42 seconds. Her achievement in that 10,000 metres was even more amazing than just breaking the record. She ran the second half of the race 11 seconds faster than the world record for 5000 metres. And she ran the final 3000 metres 5 seconds faster than the world record for that distance. In a single race, she bettered three world records. Before the start of 1993, Wang's best time for the event was 32:29.90, which she had run in Seoul the previous September. She had made a massive leap.

But it still wasn't over. That race took place on 8 September 1993. Three days later, Wang placed second in the 1500 metres to Qu Junxia, the world 3000-metre winner from Stuttgart. Qu Junxia ran 3:50.46 and broke the 13-year-old record of 3:52.47 held by Tatyana Kazankina (who was later banned for refusing a drugs test). In coming second, Wang's 3:51.92 was also under the old world record mark.

And finally, Wang was part of a mass ransacking of Tatyana Kazankina's 10-year-old record of 8:22.62 in the 3000. By the time the heats and final were over, five Chinese runners had bettered that time, and Wang had twice smashed the record. She ran 8:12.19 in a heat and then an incredible 8:06.11 in the final. The old record had been untouched for nine years. Five Chinese obliterated it.

There are bad weeks and there are good weeks for athletes . . . and there is what happened that week at the Chinese National

Games in Beijing! The seven fastest 3000-metre runs of all time in the one meet. Records were not just broken but shredded. And all by young girls from the same province, who were trained by the same coach. We learned about these feats nearly every day, and they changed the way we viewed our world as athletes. Suddenly all the parameters changed. All the targets. All our ideas of what was a good split, a good time.

It was very easy for people to point fingers, but personally I was interested. The Chinese were amazing, but there were smaller precedents. When the Kenyans started coming out of the Rift Valley they made huge inroads into world record times. Lasse Viren in 1976 did likewise in the 5000 and 10,000 metres. Grete Waitz and then Ingrid Kristiansen both knocked huge chunks off women's world records. What happened in China seemed unlikely; but it was also possible if you wanted to believe in it.

I was fascinated more than angry. I don't know how people wouldn't have been interested. Drug taking would be such a disappointing explanation for runs that were redefining the limits of women's potential on the track. If you spent your days, as I did, wondering about the limits of your own potential and about how far and how fast it was possible to run, well, the news that somebody had found a new and legal way to push the envelope seemed exciting.

It would be arrogant just to assume straight off the bat that somebody doing something better than you could do, somebody doing something different, would automatically have to be cheating. I read about and listened to what the Chinese were doing. It was strange but plausible.

Even so, the questions came. It was said that the girls were running 180 miles a week, that at times they would run a marathon a day. Yet they still had astonishing speeds as well as endurance. Doing high mileage tends to take away from your speed. Perhaps they were just physiologically different.

So many versions of the secret of their success came trickling out. Some people said that China was flooded with old East German coaches. The Chinese said that it was all down to a health tonic made from caterpillar fungus. Ma Junren said he fed the women soup made from soft-shell river turtles and a potion extracted from a worm sold in China as an aphrodisiac for men. He said that he looked at deer and at ostriches to study how they ran. Five or six times a year Ma's squad would be taken to training camps on the Tibet plateau, where they ran a full marathon distance every day at altitude.

Ma claimed he had identified the three performance 'peaks' that would come after such training: after three days, after a fortnight, and after a period of between 21 and 24 days. His runners had returned to high-altitude training straight after the Stuttgart World Championships to peak for the National Games, he said.

Most of all, though, I would love to meet those girls and talk about what their lives were like. I have nothing against the girls. If I was cheated, it was hardly by a 20-year-old girl from a remote province in China who set out to obtain steroids or whatever it took. If I was cheated, it was by a system that made those girls victims too. If I was cheated, we were all cheated.

I would love to sit down and put it all on the table and discuss what was going on. I would love to put my training notes and diaries on a table and for them to put theirs on too and to study what we all did. Swap experiences and stories.

I would like to meet Wang. I had this little rivalry with her which only existed in my head, I suppose. Same with them all. I ran and they beat me. They went and ran these superfast times. For the next year everyone was asking me about them constantly and I was always saying, 'Yep, bring them on.' There was never any show from them. I doubt if anybody was asking them about me!

I remember Wang from the Olympics in Atlanta. I was having a bad time and she was on her way to two medals but no records this time. We shook hands. She had no English and I had no Chinese but there was such friendliness in her, such goodwill in the way she looked at me and how she seemed to want to reach out and communicate. Our stories were intertwined in a way that neither of us will ever fully realize or understand. That's my memory of her: a nice girl wanting to shake hands and make further contact. We had stories we could have told each other.

I spoke to another one of them in 1997 in the World Indoors, Liu Dong. She was the girl who won the 1500 in Stuttgart. She was a Chinese team manager by then. She gave me her address. All in Chinese. I have it somewhere at home. My idea is to photocopy it and put it on an envelope and send her a Christmas card one year and see if I get a reply.

Liu Dong had got off the Ma Junren team quite early on for having long hair. One of his rules was that you had to have short hair and they all had those boyish haircuts. She was the first to go when it all broke up. There were stories of the girls having been badly treated and their prizes taken away from them. I would love to know what their lives are like now. Wang was quite young when she was famous; the last I heard, she was studying.

I would love to sit down with them. First question? I don't know. How were you all so good in 1993? What was it? Good or bad? What was the one thing that you reckon made you so good? How did you do it all without getting injured?

I don't know what their answers would be. I wanted to believe. And whatever happened, I don't think it was the girls' fault. I wanted to believe. And I still do. It has never seemed to me that it could have been easy to do everything that they did in China. People didn't make an honest effort to understand the possibility that the Chinese might have been genuine.

Those of us who can afford to, search the world for good places to train. They had it at home in this province, Lianong, apparently. They have the population. They have altitude. It is just hard for us to imagine the world they come from, but it is the same with Kenya and Ethiopia and we came to accept that. You had to factor in that maybe it was the differences, the things we didn't understand, that made them better. Maybe we just have it easier.

We train hard, but in nice parks; we wear free, state-of-the-art running shoes and we run with the back-up of so much sports science, with lots of rest and good nutrition. That's our world.

I remember when Derartu Tulu came to Europe from Ethiopia

in 2005, she came to London and she stayed with me. I took her running in the park and she couldn't believe it, how nice it all was and that we were running through this perfectly manicured park. We met some deer along the route and had to stop to chase them out of the way. Derartu was really scared. I was half scared myself; normally I would clap and they would go away, but that day they were stubborn.

My world was so strange for Derartu that day. It made me think about the assumptions we all make and the world Wang Junxia and Liu Dong came from.

It was a strange experience, losing to the Chinese. Even though I finished second in the 1500, people around Stuttgart celebrated as if I was the best in the world. I wasn't. Wang went on to become the IAAF Athlete of the Year. It wasn't a 'personality of the year' thing, just a reward for a time. There was no connection between Wang and the rest of the world.

Stuttgart was a lost opportunity for me. I was still running really well and I won the next race, and I kept winning and kept going forward. I didn't get bogged down in it. I was young. I was fascinated by the challenge of the Chinese.

So, the yes or no. Was I cheated? Were we all cheated? With a gun to my head, I would have to say, 'Yes.' There was something not quite right and I don't think it was investigated as thoroughly as it should have been. The times the Chinese girls ran, back home, in the 3000 and possibly the 10,000? Nobody is ever going to run like that. 8 minutes 6 seconds? There are definitely questions about that.

In 1993 and in the years just afterwards, I longed to race the Chinese again. That was all I wanted. If they had made a great leap forward in the possibilities for female athletes, I wanted to make it too. I picked up my training and tried to match the workloads they were doing. I could have waited around and pointed fingers at them and wasted energy being angry, but I wanted to deal with the whole thing on the track.

There were questions, and on balance 15 years later I have my doubts. Six of Ma Junren's runners were tested positive by the

Chinese themselves before Sydney 2000 and got expelled from the Olympic squad, so not everything was clean.

What makes the whole thing more suspicious as the years go by is the fact that the whole business in 1993 was never part of a progression. Those young girls running those incredible times in Beijing weren't the start of a new era. They are as much of an aberration now as they were then, when they shocked us all. If the Chinese had discovered a new type of training regime, an entirely new approach to nutrition and recovery and workload, then in time what happened in Beijing in September 1993 would have come to be seen as the start of a new era.

Instead, it all stands out just as astonishingly as it did when it happened. The nearest anybody has got this century to the 1500 metres record that the Chinese set that week was Turkey's Sureyya Ayhan, who ran 3:55.33 in Brussels in 2003. The next year she copped a two-year ban for refusing to submit to doping control. All these years, and nobody has come to within 30 seconds of Wang's 10,000-metre record.

And I suppose the question which was asked a lot back then still stands. Why did the progress of the Chinese, like that of the East Germans before them, just involve women? Women benefit much more from the use of steroids and other illegal drugs because of the lower levels of testosterone we start out with. So why were these dramatic leaps not matched, even remotely, by Chinese men?

So there are questions and doubts, but there's not as much anger there as you would think. The Chinese are part of my history, something that happened. I remember them as people I ran against on a track rather than as a conspiracy.

The Chinese, whatever their secrets were, made me better for the next two seasons. All I wanted was to meet them again and race them again and, whether they were clean or not, I wanted the chance to beat them. Anger didn't come into it. Anger was a waste of time. Still is.

I look back on those couple of years, 1992 and 1993, and I suppose I could live there forever, harvesting the regrets or the doubts. Poor Yelena Romanova, who won the gold medal that night in Barcelona, died alone in a flat in Volgograd in January 2007 at the age of 43 of causes which have never been properly explained. You can imagine the whispers.

Yelena won the gold medal that night and Tetyana Dorovskikh (also of the Unified Team and later of Ukraine) was second. Dorovskikh was a double world champion in the 1500 metres and 3000 metres in Rome in 1987 and she was the gold medal winner in the 3000 metres at the Seoul Olympics. And she finished ahead of me in second place in Barcelona in 1992. In June 1993 she tested positive for drugs and received a ban which effectively ended her career. If I wanted to make assumptions about Yelena and Tetyana I could convince myself that I should have had silver behind Angela Chalmers in Barcelona and then, with the help of a few more assumptions, have gone on to double gold in Stuttgart a year later.

That isn't the life I had, though. You run against whoever is on the track beside you. You assume that because you are clean and you have a view of how you want to be and how you want to represent yourself and your country, everyone else is clean. You have to do that or you will drive yourself mad with distraction.

You have to do your drug tests and trust to the authorities to catch the cheats and to protect you. If you spend your career being angry and suspicious and paranoid about what everybody else is doing, the pleasure will be gone. It is about racing. Or at least it always was for me. If somebody beat me when juiced with steroids or EPO or whatever, they had to live with the emptiness of that win and the fear of being caught. My fourth places in Barcelona and Stuttgart and my silver in Stuttgart, like everything else in my career, both good and bad, at least were authentic to me. I could feel each race and experience each result honestly. That's all you can do and all you can hope for.

Did what happened with the Chinese girls in 1993 cost me the Olympics in 1996? Not really. Certainly I stepped up my workload because of Stuttgart and I was better in 1994 and 1995 because of what the Chinese gave me, what they inspired me to do. Without them I would have gone along, happy to win the races. I wouldn't have raised my game. Because of them I went down the path of exploring what was possible through extreme hard work and training.

Maybe I took too much out of myself. Maybe it was all being stored up for Atlanta, but I can't blame that on the Chinese. By the end of the 1995 season I would have achieved everything in athletics except win an Olympic medal. And I knew that at that point I would have to go through everything all over again to get there and win that gold medal in Atlanta. To take care of myself properly from that point on was my responsibility. Not that of the Chinese.

Through the intensity of the whole winter and spring on the road to Atlanta I set the bar so high for myself. If I had gone into 1996 in a different frame of mind, if I had just gone in and tried to win the races one after another all the way to the Olympic podium rather than trying to beat everyone else into oblivion, I would have been better off. But I wanted to be fit enough to run like the Chinese, just in case they came back. I wanted to take chance out of the equation.

In Gothenburg in 1995, when I won the World Championship, I had a time of 14:30 in me, just in case I needed it. I won the World Championship final running well within myself. I ran 14:46.47 for the 5000 metres that night. The fastest time of the season and the third fastest of all time. By the next year I may have gone over the top and never got back to that level again.

I used up a lot of resources. I would go and go and go, and then have a big rest at the end of the season. I thought I was OK doing it that way. People train differently now. I would work myself to the bone, then rest for weeks. Nowadays people don't have complete rests but they have less intense times in between what rests they do take. I think my pattern gave me injuries and wore me down. I would stop for a month and then try to start again exactly where I had left off, only I couldn't.

None of that was the fault of the Chinese girls. When Stuttgart was over they vanished from our lives. News of their deeds reached us from Beijing, but they stopped being a reality. Five days after Stuttgart I was in Berlin and I ran 14:45.92 for the 5000 metres, the best time of the year and the third fastest of all time. I went on to win the Grand Prix final in the 3000 metres and was second in the mile. It was as if the Chinese had never happened.

Except their legacy was something I always needed, it was something to aim at, something to measure myself against. Once upon a time it was Diane McCarthy whom I targeted. And then it was Anita Philpott. At my peak it just happened to be the mirage which the Chinese left behind them in 1993; but the intensity that the shared obsession Kim and I had with running was such that I most probably would have gone down much the same path anyway. And, being me, I would probably have crashed through all the warning signs as well!

It's still a mystery what happened in August and September of 1993. I never spoke to any of them; they had no English. I knew a meet organizer at the time who lives in Cologne and whose wife is Chinese; and he went out there a couple of times to check out the scene. It remained a mystery. As years went by I appreciated that I would never get a second chance to figure it out.

Apart from the drugs, the best explanation of the Chinese times was the theory of crash training. They did so much training and then bang!, they broke down. It's physically possible, I suppose. Ever since then I trained harder each year; and today, although nobody comes near the times, athletes run more miles than ever each week.

For me, that was the first chance to make a significant impact at a major championship, and it was taken away with everyone looking on. That was a regret, and for a short time I brooded on the idea that every major championship for the rest of my career might be the same.

Now it's as if those girls never existed, except as names and numbers in the record books. I look at 8 minutes 6 seconds instead of 8 minutes 21 seconds as a world record time. There's no point in wondering why. No point in jabbing fingers and being angry.

You keep running, and the world keeps turning.

somebody like me after a scholarship to Villanova, I can hardly imagine what it must be like for a young fella from the Rift Valley.

Mike contacted Kim, who had always believed that if Kenya's athletes were to get themselves properly organized, they would have a huge impact on athletics. Two forces of nature had found each other. So, in 1990 seven Kenyans moved to Teddington, where Kim put them up. Eventually he would be renting three or four apartments which would be filled all summer long with athletes. Two of them from that first summer, William Tanui and Samson Kitur, won medals in Barcelona two years later. By then Moses Kiptanui had joined the group, and things just went from strength to strength and the stable of Kenyan runners grew and grew. Kim would take a few trips to Kenya every year to see the best of the talent coming through, and he had such a love for his job and a love of running that he spotted the best potential straight away, and the best always wanted to come back with Kim.

Kim was the first to see the need for what he did, and he was the best at doing it. As an agent he offered a service that looked after every detail, from travel and hotels to appearance money and endorsement contracts. Anything that you needed in your career but which would distract from your goal of racing very fast was looked after by Kim. A complete package. And he was very good at it and very scrupulous.

Kim became my agent as a result of my friendship with Marcus and Frank and with another Irish athlete, Gerry O'Reilly, whom I knew from my college days at Villanova. These three (and many more) were represented by Kim and, like most things in athletics at the time, the advertising worked through word of mouth.

It was suggested to me that Kim might want to represent me and that I might like to be represented by Kim. So the team that Kim already had on board sold me on the idea of having Kim as my agent and vice versa before I even met him.

I was starting on the international running scene when it was still coming out of the semi-professional era. Most agents did what they did because they liked the environment that athletes are in and they were in a position to be involved without actually running the races. Kim was operating on a whole new level.

We got on very well from the start. Kim had a great air of certainty about everything he did, and as a person to go to for advice he was great. I was living away from Cobh and from Sean Kennedy; the old training arrangement with Sean which had even got me through Villanova wasn't going to be sustainable forever. I was changing and looking for new influences. I remember asking Kim one day what he thought I should do and like ticker-tape from a machine he came out with this detailed schedule for me.

Kim and I were an 'item' and were assumed to be an item from early on, but it was different from most relationships. There was no future to it. I think we both knew it was never going to go anywhere. I don't know, maybe the relationship was convenient for us both. There was no first date, things just happen when you spend a lot of time around one person. I think our relationship developed through convenience. We travelled a lot together, ate out a lot, went to movies . . . all the things that athletes normally do between races and hard training. We had a lot in common and did a lot of the same things, travelled to the same places and were spending a lot of time together planning things.

It got to the point where we were doing the same thing a little too obsessively.

Kim was very routine in his ways. Too routine for me. He would go to the Italian place down the road and have a latte and toast. He didn't like butter so he would bring his own tub of Flora and give it to the woman in the café. She would keep Kim's Flora in the fridge for him.

We would do that all the time: go to the same place and eat the same things. There were certain times when you just wanted to do different things. It got a little like *Groundhog Day* towards the end. Something had to give, there was no other place to go, no other outlets for a while. But in the years between Barcelona and Atlanta our obsession worked well. It seemed healthy.

I had very few outside friendships. I would spend time with Alison Wyeth. We would run once a week and meet to do circuits in a gym once a week. It was a friendship that revolved around training, though. Nothing else. The only social outlet for Kim was to go to the movies. Sometimes I just wanted to do something different. I have a bit of a mad streak and sometimes I wanted to go and have a bit of fun. Anything. But it wasn't an issue. Athletics came first. We were obsessive about it. At the time it seemed right and normal to be obsessive. When you are winning races and getting better, the excitement fills a lot of other gaps that your life might have.

Did I ever stop and think that this was madness? Eating, drinking and sleeping athletics with the same person? Seeing my social circle shrink to a small group of training partners? Yes, I often questioned what I had got myself into, but it was difficult to change. Kim wasn't just my main support through training and signing racing shoe contracts, etc. I believed at the time that Kim was the only one who could make me believe in my ability as a runner. He was a good person to have in your corner, because he could influence a lot of outcomes. He would set up the races, then convince me that I could go out and win them.

I suppose every athlete needs the reassurance that they are doing the right thing. I was lucky that for training and usually for travelling I had the company of the other athletes whom Kim represented. I don't think I could've enjoyed travelling to races by myself without the great camaraderie that we had.

When I look back now, I think that I did really well to get back close to my best after the Olympics in 1996. It would have been very easy to throw it all away around that time. The training I was doing was nowhere near as good as what I had done in 1994–6.

Luckily, by that stage I would have Alan Storey as a coach, and Alan did things in a more relaxed and controlled way than Kim. In retrospect, that step down was what I needed. In those two years after the Chinese came to Stuttgart I used to run reps in training that in 1998 I would've been happy to get as a race result. Things like 8:38 for 3000 metres, followed by maybe four more efforts at the same pace, and always finishing off with a fast 400 metres.

I stepped everything up after Stuttgart, and because Kim and I shared the same perspective and aims and obsession nobody shouted stop. It might be easy in hindsight to blame Kim for that but I was as much to blame. In some ways this philosophy of more work being better was good. I always knew at race time that I could do whatever was needed – I had done it all and more in training and without the adrenalin of a race to push me along.

Basically I didn't understand training at this stage, and I believed everything was to be done fast on the track. If I couldn't do it at the speeds that Kim and I had agreed on I would come back to the track the next day and try again and again. Or I'd go to the park in the evening and run a lap of it as hard as I could. Flat out.

If I was angry or upset, the only thing that would get me back to the level was to go out and run hard. There was no stepping back or stepping away. It was as if I thought I could get unfit or slow overnight. I had to go and test myself whenever I had any doubts. If I stopped I might lose it all. Rest was never really a serious consideration. I would take a little bit of time off at the end of the season; but without the group to travel and train with, life was empty. As soon as I could, I would be back, going at full tilt. I never built up. I felt my body could take off again at the peak it had been at when I stopped training.

As well as the natural competitiveness with everyone else, Kim and I had a competitiveness with each other which drove things still further. I remember once in Melbourne we were both going through a phase when we were cycling a lot; and as cycling is very different from running in that you don't have to be super fit to go fast, just power will do, Kim realized he could challenge me on the bike – something he couldn't do when we were running. He was very competitive, which is why he was so good at representing athletes as he wanted to be the best agent out there. Anyway, on this day around Albert Park, Kim wanted to be the best cyclist and show me how good he was. He was on this super-duper racing bike he had bought, with clip-in shoes, the full racing gear, the cap, the lot. I was on a big old mountain bike, running shoes and normal T-shirt and shorts. We rode around for about two hours, killing ourselves, and I refused to give in.

Now, when you stop and think about it, is this something that a top coach should be doing to one of the best athletes in the world? Or that the athlete should be going along with? I'm not sure who was worse, me or Kim, for continuing on endlessly. I'm not sure either how it all came to an end; but I know I was back home in time to do my afternoon run, and I was so tired and sore from the bike that I really struggled badly to get through it.

It was a tough thing to do — and probably a stupid thing to do — but all I thought back then was that if it didn't kill you it would make you stronger. More was better. Higher, faster, further, and whatever would just make me better.

Some of that training with Kim was crazy. I ran world record sessions. We would build to these mad sessions. I would run 3000 metres, take two minutes recovery. Then run 2000 metres. Take another two minutes and then run 1000 metres.

In the 3000 I had to run 8:45. In the 2000 I had to run 5:40 (I would always go badly in that part). Then finally the 1000 flat out: 2:40.

We used to do it as normal, hitting the targets. I remember doing it once in Australia. Then in 1995, over at Wimbledon, with Frank and Paul Donovan to work as pacemakers. It wasn't a good day though, just not happening. I pulled out of it. I just said I couldn't do it and proceeded to go and do something else.

We all came back the next day. That sort of thing is such a big session, there are only certain times to fit it in. We came back next day at Kingston. Paul Donovan pacing me, I ran 8:38 for 3000; 2000 a little slower than target, and then the 1000 flat out. I always had this little lack of concentration in the middle section, I think it was a fear of not getting to the end. If I had been running a race that day, I could have done 14:30. In a race there are always a few laps where you lose it. I ran lots of races from the front but I was never really a front runner who got away and piled the laps on and ran everyone into the ground. I always had to save a little bit for the end.

Years later, I think, what the hell were we doing? Kim used to love it. Kim would say, 'You have to get out of the comfort zone, go beyond what people think you should do. Go beyond what are the normal and accepted training sessions.' He would always tell me to push on.

I did sessions in 1995 with the Kenyans. I'd fallen into that first in 1993 with my friend Bob Kennedy, the American runner, and did it without thinking about it the first time. The sessions were tough. Run a 400 in 60 seconds. Fine. Then run six of them in 60. One or two would go under 60. I needed to know that I could do all that in training, though. When I stood on the track in the final of the 5000 in 1995, I knew that if it was run in 14:30 I could keep up.

If there were little seeds of disaster planted in the obsessive way that myself and Kim went about the whole business of running, there were also little things which would come back on us too in terms of the world outside.

I never really enjoyed good relations with the BLE, the people who run athletics in Ireland. The name and the structure have since changed – for the better, I think – but back then they were a clique of amateurs struggling to deal with the professional side of the sport. For instance, the whole business of me living in England was an unheard-of insult to the Dublin athletics scene. Agents for Irish international athletes were viewed as having horns, tails and cloven hoofs, so the fact that I was in a relationship with one didn't help.

I was always outside the system from the start. I wasn't from Dublin. I wasn't in a club that ever took part in the national league. Ballymore Cobh was a tiny club. We had the cross-country teams and a few relay teams, but we never went off to do league finals and stuff like that. You'd read about it all in the *Irish Runner* magazine and you always wanted to be involved. Then, when you got older, you realized you were excluded and it would always have been that way anyway.

From afar you could see that they were very insular and clannish in that Dublin set. In later life I took to running with Thames Hare and Hounds in London. From the start they made me feel part of their running community. They were pleased when I turned up and did things for them, but I really enjoy anything we do as a club.

With the BLE I was studiously ignored all through my career when it came to asking me to promote our sport at home. There were things I wanted to do all along, to promote running in Ireland, but at home this distance existed between myself and the BLE. It got so that people would even say to me, before asking if I might do something in Cork, what would I want? I would generally be happy just to get home and be put up somewhere decent. That always surprised people.

I've always felt that because I went out on my own and did what I wanted to do without running things by the BLE, I was often overlooked unless I specifically put my hand up and demanded some attention or help. And when it came to doing that, I was often too stubborn or proud to put the hand up.

I think that there was an even greater stubbornness in the organization that defied any change, even when it was so obvious that changes would only be for the better.

There were nearly 50 years between Ronnie Delany's gold medal on the track and my silver medal in 2000. Back when Ronnie won his gold, I'm sure people thought the history of Irish athletics was just starting again. They would have spent a long time looking through the ranks and wondering where the next medal-winning Olympian was coming from. Nobody came through. Ronnie came from Villanova. I came from Villanova. On the track there was nothing in between really.

A lot of runners these days get more support than I ever did, which is a great thing; but that support doesn't change them as much as I changed as an athlete from 1992 to 1993. I was in at the deep end, and nobody from the BLE ever took me aside and told me they would help me to do this or to get through it. I just went for it. It was hard. It was scary. And when they came looking for their cut, it was difficult giving up some of your reward to people who treated you like an outsider.

When you went to college in America and lived in that system, firstly it was an eye-opener as regards how well-organized things could be. And, secondly, you realized you had to push the BLE to include you in things. They would forget about you. Happily.

Things have improved slowly. I am still completely outside the loop, but athletes whom I talk to say that things have got better. Over recent years there has been a lot of support, and as a result of this we are seeing athletes turning up at championships better prepared and with better support from the Irish Sports Council. These athletes are in contact with coaching staff who are now active in supporting and encouraging athletes. And Mark Carroll has been appointed to look after Irish athletes in the USA, a common-sense approach at last.

I think because I went to the USA for college and then had a coach and an agent outside Ireland, I was pushed to the edge. So instead of waiting around to be told what to do I just made plans and got myself where I needed to go as best I could. I never waited to be handed a plane ticket, I organized my own travel and I often failed to receive any reimbursement for my travel expenses. I just knew that if I waited, I might never get to a race at all. That sounds harsh, but lots of runners will remember Irish training camps which, when we arrived at them, would have a track for the sprinters and no facilities for anybody else, appalling food and bad accommodation. If you took your career seriously, you looked after your career yourself. You weren't part of the gang and if you were reasonably good they just assumed you knew what you were doing and they ignored you. We were always a group of individuals on a team. Athletes without our own coaches. You would join a team, and the team coach would be the personal coach to one or two. They would get the attention and the coaching. You looked after yourself.

You never felt there was somebody making sure there was a place to run. It was more a question of location. We went to

Portugal once and there was nowhere to run: a town, a track, but nowhere to run if you weren't a sprinter. And of course the track was filled with sprinters. We ran around the infield in the grass. That was 1987. Things changed very slowly.

In 1992 I went to another camp in Cap d'Aigue. There were some people there to run with. It was fun, way more fun than it was supposed to be. We went to the beach one day. We were out, lying by the pool then. Out of guilt we finally had to decide for ourselves that maybe we were getting a bit too much sun and a bit too little exercise.

Communications for these sort of things were always fun. Invitations would go out. 'Would you like to be part of the team! Could you fill in your details: height, weight, date of birth.' As if those details had changed since the last time you filled them all in. Inevitably, though, you would get these forms to fill in when you came back.

Food was never considered to be important. You would eat in the restaurant at the place. You had whatever they had. From a young age I always brought my own stuff and made do. I was always a bit fussy anyway. I never ate white bread, for instance. I was always on something, a fruit diet or whatever. (I still always bring a selection of tea bags and mini pots of jam. I'm always smuggling mini jam pots from the hotel breakfast tables to save for later on — the perfect size to travel with.)

I was making enough money so that I was happy. In 1993, as part of the idea of licensing the agents, a system came in where we had to pay a percentage of our earnings to the BLE. I think it was 5 per cent. I sort of objected because of their incompetence and attitude towards me, but it was just easier to pay them something every year to keep them quiet.

They weren't so quick when it came to posting money back for expenses, of course. With trips the organization was so ramshackle that I would rather get there and worry about the cost later. Much later, usually. Until recently I still had receipts pending for the Europa Cup trip to Tallinn in 1994! When Brendan Hackett took over, a couple of years ago, I finally got it back. You had to pay for everything first and then get reimbursed.

At that stage, when you are among the best in the world, maybe you don't need it, but it helps younger athletes to spend the money on proper training camps. If you are representing your country you should feel as if you are being given the best of everything. With the BLE, though, I always felt that I was on the outside and never really a part of the Irish team. There were and are definitely some good people in the sport who have always supported me, and when they were involved in the team management roles I felt more involved. Father Liam Kelleher, Sean Naughton, Georgina Drumm, Jerry Kiernan and Eamon Harvey are a few who come to mind; they always looked after the athletes' needs first. Generally, however, myself and the BLE circled round each other with suspicion and sometimes with loathing.

I persevered because I loved running for Ireland. Kim was different, though. He wasn't especially interested in the politics or the sensitivities of the BLE. If they were doing their job, that was fine and he would cooperate. If they weren't doing their job – and usually they weren't – he would just get on and look after things himself. If you had Kim's knowledge of the circuit and what other elite athletes were doing on the road to major championships, I'm sure being told by some suit in Dublin what to do was more than a little frustrating.

He was pragmatic and clear-headed about the way athletics was changing and he wanted me in the best races, running against the best opposition. What the BLE thought wasn't really a consideration for Kim. Between one thing and another I probably missed out a bit in that regard. I know that lots of decisions were made for me when I wasn't old enough to realize that it was important to do things in Ireland. Simple things: coming back for the 'Sports Star of the Year' award, or any award really. There were times when I wouldn't come back and my father or mother would go along and pick up the award.

Maybe I should have recognized the more important events that I should have been at. Especially things for Irish sportswomen. I always wanted to run the women's mini marathon. Kim would shake his head and roll his eyes, and from a professional perspective I can understand that he had good reason to. But here were Irish women doing something they wouldn't normally do, something I do every day. I wanted to be part of it and I should have pushed a little more.

So we had two cultures rubbing against each other. Kim moved in an atmosphere of ever increasing professionalism; athletics had moved so quickly from the old days of fiercely guarded corinthianism to under-the-table professionalism to the point in the early 1990s when we weren't running just for money any more at the end of a Grand Prix season. We were actually running for solid gold bars. What more vivid and vulgar symbol of the triumph of professionalism over amateurism could there have been than those shots of athletes brandishing their gold bars?

And back in Dublin the BLE were talking about club transfers and domestic meets and living in their own compact universe.

Kim, despite being an agent, wasn't too concerned about money, more about making an efficient use of the time for training which we were both obsessive about.

All through those seasons there was a very uneasy relationship between BLE and those of us athletes who were making our living on the circuit. In 1993, for instance, a couple of us opted not to run in the National Championships in Belfield in July and decided to go to a meet in Copenhagen instead. The Copenhagen meet tallied better with preparations for Stuttgart, but the BLE hit the roof. On the one hand, they said, the National Championships were the main event of Irish athletics and myself and the others had a duty to be there. On the other hand, any time we did show up at the Nationals they made absolutely no effort to promote the event, and I for one always felt most unwelcome. They wanted elite athletes to make the journey home, forgoing better races (and money) elsewhere, but when they came home they wanted us to qualify in heats along with club runners. We didn't see ourselves above club runners, but in terms of training patterns it was a disruption for professional athletes. Year after year you would come home to run in Belfield or Santry at an event which was kept almost secret, apart from the Dublin running clique. You would run around in heats in front of empty stands or vacant grassy banks and, win or lose, you would come off and get changed in an atmosphere of general hostility.

In 1993 too I had opted not to go to Toronto for the World Indoor Championships early in the season and I hadn't entered the World Cross Country Championships in Budapest. I was building for Stuttgart, I had injury problems and those events weren't in my programme. I have a long stride which isn't suited to indoor running generally (Marcus, one of the greatest indoor runners, used to say that some people just aren't meant to run indoors. I was one of those people) and I was still hurt that in 1992, when I was training for the Olympics and had yet to start properly making money as an athlete, the authorities had failed to provide a training grant yet they seemed to think they owned me. So in 1993 the BLE took offence at my schedule and it was conveyed to me that I was in their black books.

The BLE never seemed able to handle the idea of people operating and thriving outside its own little clique. In 1988 they had almost stopped athletes like Eamonn Coghlan, John Treacy, Marcus O'Sullivan and Frank O'Mara from competing in the Olympics in Seoul after a row over a Trust Fund payments scheme that Dublin had come up with.

Anyway, having missed Cork and the Nationals in 1993, the following year I was back in the National Championships. And I also ran the Cork City Sports in the Mardyke and for Ireland in the Europa Cup in Estonia. It didn't make us all one big happy family, though. The BLE were still mad. Somebody had come up with an idea whereby agents would have to sign a contract with the BLE if they were to manage the affairs of Irish runners. Running the Nationals was necessary if you were to be picked for Stuttgart, and going to Stuttgart was necessary if you wanted to run in Atlanta. Kim agreed to enter me in the races but declined to sign the contract. There was a stand-off. If I was running in the Nationals and Cork, I was complying with the BLE's wishes, and

Kim's refusal to sign a contract wasn't going to affect anyone, but it rankled with the BLE.

By 1995 storm clouds were visible. A motion was put to the BLE's annual conference in Cootehill: 'The Board shall have no dealing with people who are persona non grata with other Associations.' It was pointed out, however, what the consequences of having no dealings with Kim were, and the motion was defeated. Later on in the agenda it was noted that the BLE had in good faith signed a contract with Asics for the supply of gear for Atlanta. An impasse had arisen with the Olympic Council of Ireland, who had an arrangement that Olympic athletes would wear Reebok. Both sides were digging in.

I hardly even noticed.

8

Late in the 1994 season I think I realized that I had pushed too hard in responding to the Chinese. Sometimes your body sends you distress signals, but if your brain is stubborn enough it just overrides them. Late in the 1994 season I was just running on empty. I know when the batteries are gone because I get cold sores on my lips. I had a fairly good crop in 1994. It had been a fine season though. On a Friday night, just a week after running a new world record in the 2000 metres in Edinburgh (OK, a rarely run event but the record still stands!), I broke the 10-year-old European 3000-metre record at Crystal Palace. Twelve months previously, the time of 8 minutes 21.64 seconds would have been a world record. The Chinese had intervened since then though, and the four fastest times on record were all Chinese. I was fifth. In 1994 I ran the year's fastest times in the 1500, the mile, 2000 metres and 3000 metres, and the second fastest time in the 5000 metres.

I had enjoyed a good season, establishing myself again at the head of the pack on the circuit. I decided to keep going at the end, even when tiredness began to creep in. I won European gold in Helsinki in the 3000 metres, having decided to run in only the 3000 metres there.

Although it had been a fine season, I ran into three successive defeats on the way to Helsinki and I probably didn't arrive feeling as dominant as I should have. There were whispers about the place that I had been over-raced, having started the season with eight wins in succession.

On the day of the final I spent nearly all my time in bed resting and trying to focus on the race. That whole summer seemed to come down to races between myself and Yvonne Murray. I had been eleventh to Yvonne in the European Championships in Split four years earlier, but by the time we got to the line in Helsinki I had beaten her in our three races that season.

That August night in Helsinki had a familiar feel to it. Yvonne Murray pushed the pace out. I followed. With three laps remaining it was down to the pair of us that night. We had a 30-metre lead over the pack and we doubled it over the next 400 metres. I felt good, though. Yvonne was pushing hard, she was a great competitor like that. But I was cruising. I sat on Yvonne's shoulder till we both knew the jig was up. With 200 metres to go I put my foot down and pulled away. The time, 8 minutes 31.84 seconds, was quick for a championship final and though Yvonne was tiring at the end she was comfortable for second in 8 minutes 36.48 seconds. A few seconds further back was this Romanian girl called Gabriela Szabo. She ran 8 minutes 40.08 seconds just three weeks after winning the world junior title. One to look out for.

It seems a small enough deal now, looking back on it, and I went to Helsinki expecting to win and expected to win by others, but that was my first major championship victory. At the time it seemed like it would have to be the first of many. The World Championships would follow the next year and then the Olympics in 1996, and so on in a happy cycle. You never know what troubles are hiding behind the next tree. My body started dropping hints.

In the Grand Prix final in Paris in early September, for instance, I hurt badly. I was like one of those cartoon characters that runs out over the edge of the cliff and keeps running for a while before realizing there is nothing underneath them but a thousand feet of fresh air. In Paris I got that little bit of panic when I looked down and realized that there was nothing there. My momentum and desperation let me get a little grip on the other side with my fingernails, though.

Catherina McKiernan caught me that night in the 5000 metres but I hung on through sheer bloody-mindedness and won. You can do that when you are obsessed. You can tell yourself winning is more important than showing weakness. You can pretend to yourself that winning is a cure for even feeling weakness. I got away with it that night in Paris, but my body cried out that I was not to do that to it again. I had never felt so bad after a race. In my diary the next day I jotted down the time (15:12) and noted afterwards, '. . . not as easy as it should have been'. My body was pleading. I told it to shut up and keep quiet.

Six days later in London my body had its revenge. I went in the 1500 metres in the World Cup in London. And finished fifth. Exhausted.

And? That was Friday, 9 September. On the Sunday I did a gentle 35 minutes with Moses Kiptanui in Delhi. I ran a 1500-metre race there the following Tuesday, and then two days later ran a 5000 metres in Tokyo.

I look at the diaries from 1994 and late 1993. They tell the tale of how I responded to the Chinese. By the end of October 1993 I was up to running 100 miles a week for the first time ever. A year before that I had been running a maximum of 80 miles, but not regularly. In October the Chinese had done their wonder deeds at their National Games. Amid all the talk of caterpillars and turtles there was a persistent rumour of them doing 180 miles a week in training, and that was what interested me the most. Could it be done?

My thinking at the time in the short term was that I would do 160 kilometres a week anyway. That would be the start of my campaign to match them. So I started on a regime of at least 100 miles a week and kept going.

I remember the first time I ran 100 miles in a week; I remember knowing that I was going to crash past that milestone. At first it felt like it was an achievement. Then I had to get good at doing it. Better and better every week. Do the 100 miles. Get used to doing that. Then do more. Then do it better. Even in 1993, after the season ended for most people, I didn't let go. I was still out there, looking for whatever it would take.

In early December I ran a road race in Geneva, and then a week later I travelled to Kenya for a short while. I was a week or so out there. I went there to work at altitude, having never run at altitude in my life. We went out to this safari spot one day. Looked around but saw no wild animals other than ourselves. It was the end of a long year but I was pumping out the sessions. A 50 minutes' run in Nairobi one day, then a track session in the same afternoon, running 8 x 400 metres, all but one coming in between 62 seconds and 67 seconds.

I got injured when I came back from Kenya. My new regime worked until I started to feel the niggles. I suppose an injury was inevitable. In January I was supposed to go to North America to race indoors. Nothing happened. Still injured. I spent the month in the pool and on the Lifestep machine in the gym. I was due to be back running in March, but the injury wouldn't quit. I went to Florida in the second week in March and saw Gerard Hartmann, the physio/miracle-worker who has made such a difference to my career.

I stayed for nearly a month and, apart from a day off to spend time at the beach, just worked hard in the pool, at plyometrics (balancing the effects of contracting and expanding the muscles), on the treatment table following Gerard's orders. Just a few weeks of putting myself back together before I headed up to Philly and home from home in Haverford.

It would be hard to overstate the influence Gerard's work has had on my running. I had been to see Gerard in Florida the year before, while I was living in Philadelphia. He was in Gainesville at the time, working with a sports injuries clinic down there and really starting to establish himself.

He had his own little sideline. He worked nine-to-three at this Florida Sports Medicine place and then came back and treated his own athletes. He had this dingy little apartment and anybody who went there would stay with him in the apartment. He is good company; but even if he wasn't, the social discomfort would have been worth it. He is that good at what he does.

The week before I arrived Marcus had been down there. Eamonn Coghlan had been there. Everyone would go down there when they needed to get the engine serviced. Gerard had the only apartment in all of America without a TV in it. He had no ambition to stay in America. He just wanted to get his experience. The next year, with the Olympics looming in Atlanta, he decided to stay on.

He was becoming an increasingly important part of my career. For some reason, in athletics I've always had way more men friends than women friends. I can only talk about so many things to other girls. Marcus, Frank and Gerard are still good friends and are still the people I would look to for advice. Gerard would be the closest thing to somebody I would call up for a chat and a chance to pick his brains. I still don't know what all these questions are that go around in my brain, but I have to call people up and run things past them. Gerard has opinions about stuff, about anything. He's not afraid to tell you things. I need the reassurance of other people's opinions, and Gerard would always be frank and honest about what he saw as being good for me. On rare occasions I have gone against his advice. (In the 2002 Europeans, he advised me to concentrate on the 5000 metres as Paula Radcliffe was going to run 30 minutes in the 10,000. I took it as a challenge and went back to London and began my training regime which featured lots of 1000-metre runs in three minutes or under. I came second in the 10,000 and second in the 5000, as Gerard had predicted. He never lets me forget.)

There was a time later when Paula was at her peak, when Gerard became just as important to keeping Paula on the road as he was to keeping me going. Paula wanted to employ him solely and exclusively and would have paid him to work with her all the time. There was a lot of talk that I had a problem with the amount of work Gerard was doing for Paula. Not so. Apart from being friendly with Paula, Gerard is too much of a social animal to work for any one person full time. He couldn't cope with being with one person all the time. I remember he went to Albuquerque for nine weeks once when Paula had set up training camp there and he would be encouraging people to get down just for the company. He was edgy there.

Once I went there from Australia with an Achilles problem. I was coming back to Ireland and diverted to Albuquerque. I was happy to do it on the basis that if Gerard had no time to treat me at least he would diagnose my problem and tell me what I needed to do to get back on track. Gerard is so good at motivating me. He told me that time that I wouldn't be running for a few weeks. Told me to stay in New Mexico till the end of the week and then go home and come over to Limerick as soon as he got back home. By then I would be running again. Up to that point I had nearly thrown in the towel. I never had a problem with Paula and Gerard. I think it affected him, though. A lot of the other people whom he had helped – Elana Meyer, Bob Kennedy, Frank and others – were worried that he might put all his eggs in one basket.

Back in those years when I was pushing myself to the limit, it was all made so much easier to do because Gerard could put me or any other athlete back together again better than anybody else in the world.

I ran further and I ran faster and I healed quicker. When 1994 ended I was exhausted again but I had drained the last drop of action out of the year and out of my body. It was my nature by then to look forward to the next challenge, and 1995 would be a big year. A World Championships to shoot for.

9

I took the first day of 1995 off. A little treat, seeing that I had raced in Durham on New Year's Eve. Anyway, New Year's Day was a Sunday, which meant beginning the working year on a Monday morning. That seemed right and proper.

I worked away in London and back in Dublin and then in Cork for a week and a half, and took another day off to travel to Australia. I did a couple of sessions the day I arrived and felt tired; but I was back to half-decent shape by the weekend, and did 105 miles the following week, plus a couple of track sessions and a weights session. The first race of the year was a fairly easy 1500 metres in Brisbane in early February. Two weeks later I ran another race over the same distance in Hobart.

It was all going swimmingly until the Australian Championships in early March. I ran 4:22 for the 1500 metres in a heat on Friday night and felt awful. Next day I was a little better in the final, running 4:16. Sometimes you just have to grit your teeth and grind it out.

I was back in London as the spring softened the English weather. Back to the happy rhythms of Teddington, the daily routine: leave the bed at eight, fall into a friendly pair of running shoes. Hit the roads for 20 minutes, just a jog to jerk the sleep from heavy eyes, 20 minutes or so. Then toast and coffee. I can't do anything in the morning without a run first. It's how a day begins.

Then I prepare for the track. The track is more than 20 minutes away but my thumb just can't help pressing down on that stopwatch. I don't need to time myself running to the track. But I do. Generally I get there in 23 minutes 13 seconds, give or take a second or two to negotiate a stray dog or a little old lady.

Eleven o'clock. The track: some company, some chat. Stretching and warming up and then the hard work. Some days a 2000-

metre run followed by a 1000, followed by an 800, followed by a 600, followed by a 400, followed by a 200. Getting faster and more explosive all the time.

Other days, if I'm focusing on the 5000 metres, well then it's a big session. Then I might get one of the Kenyan athletes I am training with to act as the rabbit, setting the pace and pulling me along for a while. It's lonely out there sometimes, pounding away towards perfection, chasing the rabbit.

Running. When I run I think about races, I imagine myself into a race situation. Sometimes I just think about the act of running itself, I break the running down into all its little component parts and just try to feel the mechanics of my stride. Sometimes I am distracted and think about the afternoon to come and all the things that need doing. And the best times are when my mind seems to be wiped clean of everything. I'm not thinking at all, just feeling. That's when time goes the quickest.

Back home, I like to take a freezing cold bath. I could put more ice in it but I reckon it is cold enough. They tell me this penance is good for the legs. Sometimes I will get a massage too if the calves or thighs are feeling a little tight. Then food.

My racing weight is 8 stone 3lb (115lb, or 52kg) and doesn't vary much. Up a little in winter, down again now that it is spring-time. I'll wander out for a coffee, eating a load of bananas along the way. Food is fuel really. I don't worry about it too much. When I was a girl back in Cobh, I grew tall when I was quite young and never carried much by way of weight. In school I was slightly long and gawky at a time when most girls would prefer to be a little smaller and curvier. I was never much of a dancing queen on the Cobh disco circuit; but I remember the odd visit with me bopping awkwardly with lethal elbows and my head and shoulders sticking out above the crowd.

A body like mine seemed to make best sense when I was running. I had all the usual bits and pieces yet they seemed configured for running. Running is when I am most comfortable in my skin.

I might have coffee and put in a couple of hours chatting with some other athletes. Teddington is like a mini Olympic village in that sense. Other days, if there is nobody around I will stay at home and read or talk to home on the phone. It all amounts to killing time between runs, really.

On a typical evening, at 6 p.m. a bunch of us will gather at the gates to Bushy Park for a gentle evening jog. The others like to chat and laugh and run at talking pace, but even though I will chat I have to be competitive. I can remember some of those evening runs when there was no pressure on the amount of time or pace you were running. We were running along, reciting lines from the recently released video *The Van*, an adaptation of a Roddy Doyle book. Marcus, Frank, Paul Donovan and myself, all acting out the different characters and laughing so hard we could hardly walk, let alone run. One line I remember clearly had us in tears and at a standstill: '. . . a bleeding Slut . . . what are ya?' Little did I know, these words would come back to haunt me in 1999.

These are the runs that brought relief to the daily grind, these were the runs that I looked forward to. I counted the miles in my diary; but the enjoyment was there, so the effort was minimal. This was the key to running a lot of miles; sometimes you have to back down and get the run done with as little effort as possible and be ready for the Big Session later in the week.

One afternoon I came down to Bushy Park on the bike and took a spin along the perimeter fence. I took note of all the milestones. Made the park into a track for myself, filled with little features which tell me how far I have gone and how quickly I should be going. So, one mile out is marked by a tree which stands by the cricket pitch and sticks out a little bit. You'd have to see it to know, really. Two miles, and you sail past a big tree before the bridge. Three miles? Well, a tree after a big creek marks the spot. Loop around and the four-mile mark is three small trees standing in the company of one big tree. Five miles is a special landmark: two tall trees facing each other so that in your mind you are running through a winning tape. I like that one. The six-mile spot is just at the entrance to another cricket field. Seven is back at the gate, and then home.

Because I have everything mapped out in my head we always have to run in the same direction. I don't like going the other way around. I can't go fast if I'm not going past my markers. Once we are settled and off, we go at talking speed and sometimes a bit faster. It's strange. We pass people and they are going as fast as they can run and we sail past, chatting away. We were all put together for this stuff.

Finally home again. Hundreds of sit-ups in front of the television. High knees and hops and bounds, and maybe some fast strides out on the grass. That's a working day.

Then it starts, the track hopping. Moscow. Tallinn. Cork. Gateshead. Dublin. Nice. Oslo. Crystal Palace, and so on. The road to Gothenburg and the World Championships.

I love this part of the year. Racing. Racing. Racing, and racing some more. You run races as part of your training. You just maintain the level of fitness which you ground out before in the springtime. Every race tells you a story about where you are. A modest 1500 metres (4:17) in Moscow in early June to an Irish record (3:58.8) in Monaco in late July.

The summer unravels like a game of cat and mouse. All the top runners watching one another, seeing who is going well, trying to work out which races they will enter in Gothenburg, trying to get a little psychological edge. I am hovering between the 1500 metres or the 5000 metres, eyeing the others, knowing they are eyeing me.

We play games. Who can tough one another out. I am going well at 5000 metres for instance. In June I do a lot of track work. In mid June I do a session at the track with the help of Paul Donovan. He is in London, earning some money pacing races, enjoying a session at the Wimbledon track with me. 5 x 1000-metre runs with two minutes between each run. The times are 2:48 . . . 2:49 . . . 2:50 . . . 2:51 . . . 2:53. Three weeks later at the beginning of July it pays off.

We are to race on a Friday night at Crystal Palace, Fernanda Ribeiro of Portugal and me. Provided the Chinese don't materialize out of thin air, the two of us are the favourites for the 5000 metres if we both enter. Ribeiro would like to scare me off into concentrating on the 1500. I would like her to go away and just run the 10,000 in Gothenburg. She is the European 10,000-metre Champion. She should settle for the longer journey.

Conditions are unnerving. Ribeiro ups the ante and makes a big deal about taking the pre-race initiative. She announces that she is making a world record bid and goes about setting the tasks and times for the pacemakers. This is like slapping me in the face with a pair of gloves. In public. It is a challenge and a warning.

I'm the European 3000-metre champ and am unbeaten at the distance this year. I'm also unbeaten at 5000 metres. So Ribeiro is challenging my place in our world. I think she has made a mistake. I don't go out much, but I am a student of athletics. I clock and watch my rivals; I absorb the times of every relevant race at every decent meet. I keep asking till I find out the splits and I know the last-lap times. I am looking for little cracks of vulnerability and areas of stress. I'm confident and strong at the moment. Laying down challenges to me is a dangerous business.

I was sure I was going to run really well at Crystal Palace. I set myself a target for a really blistering opening 3000 metres. Hoped to go out in 8:45 straight away on the night, though my legs told me this wasn't a possibility. I knew I would have to change plan. My legs kept warning me off. So it became a matter of just staying in and winning the race. I don't know why.

I think maybe I was just nervous in Crystal Palace. The stakes went up. The field was high quality. I was too anxious to show something. I didn't want anybody to have the impression that I don't like the 5000 metres as much as I want them to think that I like it.

In the end I ground it out with the fifth fastest 5000 metres in history, 14:47.65. Ribeiro watched from behind. It was a win for me. Yet I didn't feel as great as I should have done, I kept having to tell myself that a win is a win.

These are the mysteries of running, tracing the threads which join the mind and the body. Wondering why sometimes the dots just don't join. Some days you have it, some days you don't. Some days you set out for greatness and settle for bloody-mindedness. Some days you set out to make an impression on the clock and settle for making an impression on your rivals.

And sometimes you get kicked back. Not long after the race in Crystal Palace, Ribeiro went to Hechtel in Belgium and set a new world record for the 5000 metres. Point made and accepted. We will both be in the 5000-metre field in Gothenburg.

Fast forward.

So I am ready. I have had my coffee and bananas, my gallons of water. I have had a light run for the benefit of the legs. I'm primed and ready and waiting. I hate waiting.

I enjoy routine. I depend on the discipline it imposes and the mental comforts it brings. Every night before a race I like to lay my gear out, put my shoes neat and tidy beneath a chair, ready to go. I hate interruptions, distractions, upsets. If there is a problem I just have to find somebody who can sort it out for me.

Grand Prix races are always in the evening time. You change your rhythms for championships. At a Grand Prix on race day I'll doze till ten. Then eat toast, drink coffee and devour bananas. Have a short run before lunch, which is usually rice and bread. I like to take lunch seven hours before a race. In hot weather, I drink water practically all day long. I might eat again five hours before a race, just to fend off any hunger later on. Then I'll relax down and flick through a magazine for the afternoon. Two hours before the race I usually hit the track, ready to go.

Championships are different. Today in Gothenburg we are about three hours ahead of the usual schedule, so today has been a telescoped version of so many other days. I spent the afternoon watching the men's marathon on television and wishing the time away.

Half an hour before race time and counting. Any doubts in my head now could be fatal. It's too late for cures or miracles. On the warm-up track the rest of the 5000-metre field are jogging and stretching and strutting. I go through my own routine. The stretches, the laps, the high steps, the search for the right feel. I try to give off a look of supreme confidence. In here we can sense weakness.

The gang is all here. Fernanda Ribeiro, the dark Portuguese runner I have been duelling with. Zahra Ouaziz, the Moroccan outsider. Gabriela Szabo, who is starting to turn up everywhere. Paula Radcliffe, who hasn't yet found her event. The Kenyans, Sally and Florence Barsosio and Rose Cheruiyot. The little Swede, Sara Wedlund, and my old friend Gina Procaccio.

We are all circling one another. Pretending we have never met. Putting our race faces on. Bullet-proof!

With 40 minutes to go I nip into one of the line of brown portakabins in a corner of the field and change into my Irish vest and shorts. Tick, tick, tick. With 30 minutes to go I am gathering up my bits and pieces and collecting my thoughts.

The last-call sign is flashing insistently above the warm-up track now. Kim comes over to pin my number (495) to my back. We say our goodbyes, he reminds me what I have to do. I head down the little enclosed avenue that we must parade through like racehorses as we head towards the Ullevi Stadium.

Focus. Focus. Focus. Under the stand on this side of the stadium there is an area where we will meet the media afterwards as winners or losers. There is a holding room where we gather until we are let out on to the track. In here we put our belongings into baskets which have our numbers on them. In here you can hear every pulsebeat. You can keep your head down and avoid eye contact. Or give the impression that this is the place in the world where you would most like to be.

I am first out on the track when the hurdles are cleared away after the men's 110-metre heats. A quick warm-up to get the engine ticking again. When I line up on the white line, Fernanda Ribeiro is right beside me, touching shoulders. No thoughts now. Just the track ahead. Waiting for the crack of the pistol.

Gabriela Szabo, the (increasingly pesky!) Romanian, has pushed the pace early. For a championship race it's a very fast first lap. Sara Wedlund, the little Swede who looks like the Milky Bar kid with her blonde hair and spectacles, makes the occasional little surge, egged on by the home crowd. She did the same in the heats, made a break for it in my heat. I had to track her down and put her away.

Ribeiro waits and waits. So do I. Lap after lap, just watching each other.

As we get closer and closer to the finish, 1000 metres, 800, 600, 450 and so on, I get more confident. We head into the last lap. Now it is a game of who has the nerve to wait the longest. Ribeiro knows if it gets to the last 200 metres she is mine. It's her move.

She makes her play approaching the start of the final lap. There are just three of us now: me, Ribeiro and Zahra Ouaziz, the Moroccan girl.

When she goes I just stay with Ribeiro. It's important for me to get right in behind her when she goes. I'm there, staring at her number now, and she knows I am there. I never let her get any distance away now, not more than a yard. And I just wait. She knows and I know.

At the 250-metre mark I move outside her and stretch my legs. I know almost straight away that she has no response. 200 metres to go comes so quickly, by now I am just going for the line. Nothing is going to stop me. My race plan has been to do whatever it takes to be World Champion. The most important thing was to win the race. I knew all along that I wouldn't know what I would feel like if I hadn't come first.

I win in 14:46.47. Ribeiro is two seconds behind. Tonight, though, I had 14:30 in me if I needed it. I'm the first ever women's 5000-metre World Champion.

We would all like to be remembered. After Barcelona, and more so after Stuttgart, I had decided to keep on going, working harder and harder, getting a bit faster all the time, always working harder. I wanted to be the best. To get the best from myself. That's why I had done it all. A little slot with my name engraved in the history books.

The joy is brief. I'm an awkward winner. Not quite sure what to do with my arms. You have to run around the track and get it over with. I never looked forward to it. It's awkward and embarrassing. And anyway today I run straight into trouble on my lap of honour in the Ullevi Stadium.

My father, who has mastered the art of invisibility when it comes to stewards and security guards, was right down at the fence when I started the lap. If he was in the media zone, the athletes' area, the drug-testing control area or on the medal podium, I wouldn't have been surprised.

I went to him, we embraced and then I jumped down to the track. I left him with his Irish flag, I was sure to pick up another one along the way. Sure enough, somebody else has given me an Irish flag which was attached to what felt like a telegraph pole. It was a labour of Hercules just to lift it. I put that down after a short while and went off on a happy lap of honour. I had no idea I had disappointed everybody, even at the end when the photographers handed me a tiny Irish flag to be photographed with. The impact was gone by then apparently and they were running already with the story.

At the press conference afterwards I am asked about the flag business. Paul Kimmage of the *Sunday Tribune* asked the question and I couldn't believe it was an issue. I was really upset after it. People were saying it to me. I was explaining I didn't mean that. The emotion came then.

And people were pulling me this way and that, telling me that I had to do this television interview with John Treacy next. So I had to compose myself. And of course John, well intentioned as ever, turns up with an Irish hat for me to wear. Damage limitation! This makes me more upset. I don't want to have to perform some corny act to prove to everybody that I love my country. I feel as if I can't talk at all now. I don't want to appear upset, having just won a gold medal. It's a much bigger issue than it should have been.

Kim, of course, cannot understand any of this the way an Irish person would understand it. His head is full of the race and the times and the splits. A 61-second last lap! I'm sure John Treacy spoke to him and told him that this was important. John would have been on top of everything like that. I was so upset now that I just didn't want to talk. John was gently saying, 'You must do this, you must do that.' We get it done, me holding the hat, and it's a weight off my shoulders to have it done.

But at the same time it lingered on. Shortly after Gothenburg I won in Berlin. I'm setting off on a lap of honour and somebody threw a tricolour to my feet. Oh god. This is only a Grand Prix race! But do I ignore the flag and risk being lynched? So I pick it up and do a lap of Hitler's old stadium with my tricolour, all the other athletes looking at me as if I have lost my reason. Poor Sonia! Look at her, she thinks she has won the Olympics!

There were a few letters, of course. The patriots. My parents got most of them. They went on for a while. I even got one years later in Sydney telling me that I was a traitor. 'Dear Ms Traitor'.

I had quite a few traitor letters. They'd come on these little scraps of paper. This one came in through the village office in Sydney. 'Dear Ms Traitor. You don't deserve to run for Ireland.'

People are more open-minded about these things now. At the time I think it meant more to Irish people. A gap of 10 or 15 years makes a difference. Folk understand better now why people go abroad for their sport. The economy is so much better that it is more accepted. It's not an insult if you run for Ireland but forget to do the symbolism at the end.

It was hard to explain at the time, though. I always tried not to be too emotional about the whole thing, especially when I won. In Gothenburg I was the favourite. I was going to win anyway. I had planned to win. I have another race next week. That's where my mind was. Suddenly I had a flag that was tied on to a big tree branch or something. It was seriously heavy. You cross the line, your arms are really tired. I'd said to myself, there was no way I could get around with this burden. What do I do with it? Do I find whoever handed it to me and try to give it back? You just live in the moment. It wasn't supposed to be a national insult.

At that time not everybody carried flags around the stadium, but people wrote about it and questioned the whole thing.

And part of it was my fault. I thought the racing was enough.

It took till 1998 for me to realize that the flag and the lap of honour are such a big part of connecting with the people who are watching you and supporting you.

In 2006 I saw Derval O'Rourke winning silver in the European Championships. Derval was jumping up and down with the flag afterwards. That's the emotion that most people like better than the race itself. It took me a while to get that, though!

Looking back, Gothenburg should have been a halting point for me. But I was obsessed with working harder and going harder. I announced in the immediate aftermath that I was officially training for Atlanta now.

It is hard to describe my mindset now. On 12 August I won the World 5000-metre Championship. I recorded how I felt in my diary, noted that I did a 12-minute warm-down underneath the stadium ('very warm . . . but nice').

Next morning I did 55 minutes' easy running in the park and on the Monday I got up at 7.30 a.m. and did some easy jogging and then caught a plane to Zurich. In Zurich I did a 43-minute run that afternoon. I wrote that I felt OK after the first 10 minutes. On Wednesday night I ran in Zurich (3000 metres in 8:27.51, with a 62-second last lap). On Thursday morning I was 'a little bit tired' running 35 minutes in Zurich, but I ran another 20 minutes when I got to Cologne that evening. On Friday I ran the mile race at the Cologne meet (winning and 'feeling good' in a time of 4:24 with a last 200 metres in 27.7). Next day, back in London, I did an hour and 25 minutes.

I stayed at home there till Wednesday, when I travelled to Brussels, where I was hot and dizzy during the 5000 metres on Friday night. Still, I ran back to the hotel immediately afterwards. I felt better on Sunday back in London though, leading the 3000 metres from the very start at Crystal Palace. And so on and on and on. I won in Berlin then straight away took a seven-hour trip to Rieti. There I was distracted and nearly beaten in the mile by the pacemaker who was told I wanted to break the world record . . . it was a bit late in the year for world records; still, on I go to

Rome, then to Monte Carlo where, still not feeling well, I ran a 3000 metres on the Saturday night and then flew to Hong Kong next morning before heading to Tokyo two days later.

I won the 5000 metres on a Friday night and then did 10 miles through Tokyo next morning before flying four hours to Hong Kong and then another 12.5 hours to Johannesburg and then yet another two hours down to Cape Town. I arrived in Cape Town at 9.30 a.m. and went running that afternoon.

I had a week in South Africa, staying with Elana Meyer in Stellenbosch, and then a race in Johannesburg on Sunday, and then straight to the airport from the track. Two days in London. Five in Ireland.

And then off to Haverford again. Back to work. Hi-ho, hi-ho.

Some of my diary entries that autumn just read 'felt pretty horrible' . . . 'felt terrible'. I wrote those words, but with Atlanta looming on a not so distant hill I viewed the feelings they described as signs of weakness.

10

Maybe I was pushing too hard and heading towards disaster at the time; but I think they were good for me, those few years when I won everything and did a good impression of being invincible.

It left something behind at least. A record, a bit of a legacy. I won on tracks all over Europe. Took medals away and left good times behind at the great race meetings. I was Grand Prix champion for four years in a row.

It would be hard to do all that now, hard to get that range into a career. I think the races now have more depth. It would be much more difficult to win that number of races; not many athletes would even think about running that many races today. If I wasn't winning pretty much every week it would have been hard for me to keep doing them myself. Athletes make a lot of money at the road races these days, but to do well there or on the circuit you can't be in it for the money. You won't have the same commitment to it if you are out there just for the money.

That's why some people cheat, I reckon. It's not a journey for them. There is no love or obsession to carry them through half a lifetime of just running and being fascinated by exploring their natural limits. They take the money and the brief flash of glory, and they run. If you are in it for life, it doesn't really matter if there is money there or not. You can have what you love as your job. Not many athletes whom I like and respect would know a lot about their money. They don't know the financial difference between running here and running there. They chase the races and they chase the times and they chase their rivals and they chase that idea they have of their own limits. What happens in the bank account is a mystery.

In those good years Kim would give me information sheets

on appearance fees and prize money, etc. He was efficient and scrupulous and trustworthy and I never paid that much attention. The money was always there. Everything was always on my statement, all neat and tidy and above board at the end of the year. Never a worry. If you are going to live and love the life of an athlete, that's the way to do it.

Back then, when athletics was going well and TV money was pouring in, nearly everything was paid in US dollars. When the euro came in they went to paying euros. Athletes complained for a reason that even they themselves weren't quite sure about. So they went back to the dollars when they should have stuck with euros. The most I ever got, so far as I know or remember, was between $15,000 and $20,000 for turning up at a track race. Then there were bonuses for winning, bonuses for times, prize money, etc. And something from Nike or Reebok, whichever shoe company I was with at the time.

The shoe people give you a base payment, a fixed bonus schedule which everyone gets. $50,000 for the Olympics, the World Championships or whatever big event is on the calendar, and then different bonuses for road races, track races, Golden League Grand Prix races, world records, European records, Irish records, etc. It is all laid out there. In shoe company terms, a Paula Radcliffe gold medal has the same value as some unheard-of Chinese girl winning the gold medal. The payout is the same to everyone.

You would have a rollover element built into your contract though, with your base and bonuses rolling over for the following year. For the shoe people you have to do certain appearances and run in certain races. The gear keeps flowing in. They send you a pack in the summer and winter. The amount they assign to you, there is no way you could use it all. I have a garage full of shoes. Loads of stuff you would never wear. Everything that comes out they send you some of. I keep them for the future or give them away. If you are my size, you get Christmas presents of running shoes year in and year out!

Tracksuits, shorts and T-shirts arrive by the shed-load. You have your favourites that you never want to get rid of, and the rest of the stuff is just clutter. I have a house full of it and I still have my small few favourites that I wash every week.

They send you every new style of shoe. You might not like them. I'm a fan of the Pegasus, for instance. Some new-style Pegasus shoes will arrive in a big box. I'll try a pair and decide I prefer the old style. So I just call up and say I need the 2006 Pegasus instead, thanks. And a big box of them will arrive. And they will keep arriving. Then you might decide one day that you like the new ones – and they will keep coming too.

In exchange, you run in a few races that they want you to run in and you do whatever jobs they need you to do. I quite like the little jobs they get you to do. They treat you well and it gives you a bit of variety in life. You do everything from store openings and visits to photo shoots. I've cut ribbons and I've been dragged around Dallas in supermarket trolleys as people filmed me for an ad. I've spent time in Paris trying to look either interested or interesting as they photographed me. All good diversion.

I have no idea which was the best year financially. The shoe contracts and so on always went straight into pension funds for the future. Apart from 1992 and 1993, when I first got money from America through Reebok, I don't think I have ever spent any of that money. It's in banks somewhere.

I know that the good years I had on the circuit were coincidentally good years for athletics. The sport has all but disappeared off the TV now, but at that time television money was flooding in and the big meets, especially Oslo, Zurich, Brussels, Berlin and the Grand Prix final, were massive events.

If there is TV money, there is endorsement money and appearance money and kit money. I was lucky that I came along at that time, and I was lucky that I had Kim looking after my interests, both short term and long term.

Middle-distance running didn't get tainted by drugs as badly or as quickly as sprinting did, and, like Yvonne Murray and Liz McColgan before us, I benefited from being a recognizable face in a decent market. Television and media have a tendency to dismiss all Kenyan runners as 'the Kenyans' or a group of Ethiopian and Kenyan runners as 'the Africans'. If they saw myself and Yvonne leading a race though, we wouldn't be 'the Europeans', we would be Sonia O'Sullivan and Yvonne Murray.

People who love running could recognize Moses Kiptanui or Derartu Tulu on a poster or in a picture, but I was one of the few who benefited from a spill-over into the mainstream. Even now people occasionally come up to me and say, 'Aren't you that runner?' Sometimes they will think that I am Liz McColgan or Yvonne Murray, but at a time when most people would be hard pressed to name a decent women's 5000-metre runner, it is a sign of the exposure we got.

I would be lucky too in that when my career hit a low point, or a whole series of low points, I suppose, the commercial arrangements were changing anyway. By 1997 Reebok, whom I had been with since the start, had decided to restructure their approach to endorsements; and anyway my contract had ended so I was free to switch to Nike.

Kim created or Nike offered (I am not sure which) a deal with bonuses for world and European titles. This was at a time when it must have seemed doubtful that I would ever be competing for either again. So it all worked out well without me ever having to worry about that aspect of my career.

I worked hard through 1994 and 1995 and, though I would often say to journalists that all I was interested in was the next race or the next championships, that was just a device to take the pressure off myself. Journalists wanted to talk to me about the next Olympics. Everyone did. If you aren't interested in athletics in an absorbed, nitty-gritty sort of way, well the Olympic Games are all that matter. In the real world outside athletics, being ranked world number one is an achievement, yes; but mainly it is seen as being a good thing in terms of your chances of getting an Olympic medal. The Olympics distort everything we do.

Moses knows. One of my great friends among the Kenyan crew in Teddington was Moses Kiptanui. Moses was one of the greatest 3000-metre steeplechasers ever. He was the number one ranked athlete from 1991 to 1995 and he won gold at the World Championships in 1991, 1993 and 1995. Moses was also the first man ever to run a 3000-metre steeplechase in under 8 minutes.

In 1992 in Nairobi, poor Moses, despite being World Champion, failed to qualify for Kenya at the National Olympic Trials. He missed the Barcelona Games. He ended up with a silver medal in Atlanta in 1996, and that was his Olympic record. To those who knew what he did, Moses was one of the all-time greats. In the place where everybody looks for greatness, however, he ended up without an Olympic gold. The Olympics are where it is at for your piece of history, for your pride, for your legacy, for your commercial value, for your own peace of mind.

When we are on the circuit, we love the buzz of our own rivalries and competition. A race on a damp night in Hengelo can assume great meaning for us because of the politics and personal rivalries in our little world. But for the millions who sit in their armchairs and come to athletics only when it interests them, the Olympics are the be-all and end-all. And the funny thing is, we all buy into that.

Journalists used to ask us in the run-up to the Olympics, 'So, if you could have one or the other, a world record or an Olympic gold, which would you choose?' And the athlete and competitor in you thinks, a world record that lasted would rub everyone's nose in it. A world record would deflate everybody else. But hey? An Olympic gold? You don't have to worry about anybody else. It's all over. You have it. The others don't. You will always have it.

Look at Ronnie Delany. An Olympic gold for Ireland in 1956 and he is still loved for it more than 50 years later. Some people know that Ronnie went to Villanova. Nobody knows what the rest of his running career was like, but everybody in Ireland knows that Ronnie Delany won gold in Melbourne in 1956 and fell to his knees in thanks.

So listen. When the World Championships in Gothenburg finished, when you put the medal in the box and made the arrangements to have the car you won shipped home or sold, you were happy and satisfied – but something else too. Wary.

Months. Weeks. Days left to the Olympics. So few days you could count them. And now that you were World Champion, your head was way above the parapet waiting to be blown away. There was Diane McCarthy and then Anita Philpott, and so on and on, rivals you could take the measure of and catch. You are the one everyone is measuring. You are the World Champion, and those two words are exciting and in some way fulfilling, but when you see them after your name you know that they just ain't the same thing as Olympic Champion.

Ask Eamonn. When I was growing up, Eamonn Coghlan was perhaps Ireland's greatest athlete. A Villanova man, he won the 5000 metres at the 1983 World Championships. He was criticized at home for the style of his celebration coming down the home lap. A bit too full of himself, people thought. Especially considering how he had been fourth in the previous two Olympic finals. Eamonn had won silver at the 1978 Europeans, finishing only behind the great Steve Ovett. He was one of the greatest indoor runners ever to grace the boards in the States. And yet at home he is known only for two fourth places in the Olympics.

It's like a club. The career of Hicham El Guerrouj seemed to be a cruel joke until at last he won his Olympic gold in 2004. Had he not won, he would have been chairman of the club. Among the members are: Ron Clarke, 17 world records set and no Olympic gold. Paul Tergat, probably the greatest cross-country runner ever, but no gold at the Games. Wilson Kipketer, Jim Ryun, Daniel Komen, even John Landy, who was second to Roger Bannister (no medal) in the miracle mile in 1954 but third to Ronnie in the Melbourne Games two years later. Not fulfilled. Lifetime member of the club. It's not fair, but life isn't fair!

When I was a kid running the fields of Cobh or a young athlete pounding the miles on my own in Villanova, the soundtrack running in my head most often was the commentary to an Olympic final.

I spent the summer at home in Cork in 1992 and every question was about the Olympics. We hate it and love it. We deny it but accept it. The Olympics are the Big Show. The Brass Ring.

Whatever. They are what we are judged by now and for always. I could set up a table on a street in Cobh in the run-up to any other major championship and people would stop to talk about the weather.

So we left Gothenburg and lived out the rest of the season, but by then our heads were all turned towards Atlanta, our gazes so fixed that we had cricks in our necks as we went about our daily business.

Races were no longer just races; they were the road to the Olympics. Injuries were no longer injuries; they were imperilling your Olympic chances. Days were no longer just days; they were time slipping away before the Games began.

Nobody died.

There were the tears and grief, and my career burst at the seams just when I had hoped to stand up wearing that same career as the robe of a worthy Olympic Champion. But nobody died.

I failed to even finish my 5000-metre final. I vanished down a tunnel and away off in tears into the warm Atlanta night. My armour of invincibility got left behind for somebody else to pick up.

And that was the Atlanta Olympics for me. There was much else, but if you want the condensed version of the highlights reel, the bit that everybody remembers is me disappearing down the tunnel with 900 metres to go in an Olympic final. And my dad, back to the wall, surrounded by media and hurting like hell but saying those perfect words. Nobody died.

I knew perhaps that disaster was coming, but there was nothing specifically wrong. Just an absence of the comfort I always felt when running. There was something tugging at the sleeve of my confidence on the road to Atlanta. A little whisper in my ear every now and then. A few training sessions at the track in Philly which just broke down. I told myself to relax. Marcus, who was there with me, told me to relax. There were a few sessions with Kim when I disagreed with what we were proposing to do.

My training diary from the time I got back to Haverford in mid July to the wind-down towards the Games tells the story of my body being in trouble and me trying not to make a big deal of it. I had struggled in my last race in Europe, a 5000 metres in London, but I did the usual. Gritted my teeth and made the bad feeling go away.

I ran back to the hotel in Croydon afterwards but I felt all wrong after it. I was beginning to have some doubts and worries. I was questioning everything. I wasn't happy with anything I was coming up with.

A lot of it could have been just me, I decided. I wasn't asking the right questions. Instead of going to ask the right questions of anyone who could answer them I decided to bury it all in my head.

And why not? This was it. Barcelona had been all a bonus. A novelty. This was the prime work of my career, pressing home for the reward for three years at the top. This time was for winning. Wang Junxia was to be there! Perfect. The moment I had waited on for three years. Throwing myself against her excellence. I wanted her there. Others were nervy. Fernanda Ribeiro, Julia Vaquero and Derartu Tulu all ruled themselves out of the 5000 metres on the way to Atlanta. This was my time. If only somebody would alert my body.

Kim was setting the training programme meanwhile and telling me what to do. I was arguing over things. He was saying, 'This is what you did before. Why worry?'

People say if I had had more blood tests done and had gone for medical check-ups. Maybe I was run down. There should have been indicators that tests would have picked up. But when you are a favourite for the Olympics, everyone wants something. Press conferences. Photos. Interviews. You are always rushing about doing something. Removing yourself for tests which might lead to more tests which might lead to having to take a rest which might lead to all your rivals knowing and smiling to themselves? Well, it is easier to push on and hope that the intensity of being at the Olympics will carry you through.

You can't pretend all day every day, though. On 19 July I was complaining to the diary that things were very hot and humid and that I didn't feel too good. Two days later, the same thing. A track session. Didn't feel too good. No concentration.

Things going on in my head and things going on in my body.

Marcus said, 'Relax, though.' Good idea. I relaxed and although I was feeling bad I decided to keep it to myself. When you have a problem and you share it, it gets to be a bigger problem. Everyone wants to contribute. Everyone gets involved. I kept my mouth shut. It was a problem, but by keeping it to myself I thought I would stop it from becoming a crisis.

We watched most of the first week of the Olympics in Philadelphia. Watched Michelle Smith winning those golds. People often asked afterwards, was I jealous? Did I see her as stealing my thunder? To be honest, we watched and laughed and debated all the time, looking at the size she was compared to previous Olympics we had been at with her. I didn't make any judgements, but for me the Olympics are athletics. An Irish track medal would weigh differently from any number of medals in any other events.

We got down to Atlanta on a Tuesday, with the heats for the 5000 due to take place on Friday. The first day there, Kim brought me to a Reebok press conference. I sang a happy song for everybody. We were staying in a nice house out in Buckhead, a wealthy suburb of Atlanta, about seven miles from the stadium, which was downtown.

A lot was made by the BLE later about the fact that I stayed in a house instead of at the Olympic village. I'm not sure why. The Olympic village is a nice idea, but if you are a serious athlete hoping to get everything right it's not the place you should be.

You spend all year doing everything just right. You get your rest periods, your routine, your circadian rhythms. You sleep in hotel rooms and establish your own routines, following the same pattern wherever you go. The key is: no surprises. And then, when it comes to the biggest event of your life, you bunk in with everyone else, in a village teeming with thousands of young athletes. Some of them are very serious about what they are doing, but some are along for the experience and the party. Some of them are disruptive and, as the events end, more and more of them are merrily disruptive. The athletics events start in the second week of the Games. By then, lots and lots of the Olympic programme is finished with. Thousands of athletes are wandering about with nothing to do other than party with each other, have a few drinks together and, more often than not, stay out all night, coming back with lots of loud voices, giggling and banging doors. And amid all this you are supposed to put your finger to your lips and say, 'Sssssh! Trying to get some sleep here!' Life isn't like that!

The 5000-metre heat in Atlanta was two days before the final. It was the same story as Gothenburg the year before. Wedlund, the little Milky Bar kid, went out ahead, hoping to lose everyone. Nothing scary. In Gothenburg I had burned her with a 28-second final 200 metres. Now I had hardly enough energy to catch her.

Winning the heat took a lot out of me, but I had to show how competitive I was. You have to dig it out and show everybody that you are strong and are not there to be picked off. That effort took a lot more out of me than it should have. However, that heat isn't remembered in Ireland for me catching Sara Wedlund and qualifying for the 5000-metre final.

The row between the BLE and the Olympic Council of Ireland over what gear the Irish athletes were to wear in Atlanta had rumbled on for a year. The details are too boring to rehash, but the OCI felt that the Olympics was their show and they had the right to make contracts for the gear the Irish team would wear. They signed with Reebok. The BLE felt the same about their rights. They signed with Asics.

I believed and I still believe that the OCI were right and that they were proved to be right afterwards. At the time though, I didn't care too much. I had had a relationship with Reebok since college and they had always been good to me; but, given the choice, I preferred the cut and feel of the Reebok gear. I had no stronger feelings than that. I am an athlete, not a politician.

Earlier in the year Reebok had sent me gear for the Olympics. I did a photo shoot in Dallas and some TV commercials wearing it. I liked the stuff they gave me. I heard nothing from the BLE about it, even when I wore it for the races at the Cork City Sports and then for the National Championships. Not even an official coming past and saying, 'Oh, by the way, Sonia, you can't wear Reebok at the Games.'

There was no financial incentive to wear Reebok in Atlanta. When you sign a contract with a shoe company, you sign to wear the gear at interviews and PR events and so on. You wear their shoes on the track. The bonus money is for winning a medal. It's the same for everybody.

This was the Olympics. I wanted everything about the preparation to be right. I was told and Kim was told that either set of gear would be satisfactory, but I had suspected, given the history of my relationship with the BLE, that things weren't going to go smoothly. Kim advised me to bring both sets of gear to the stadium. I did, and I wore the Reebok gear.

Just as we were in the holding area waiting to go out, I was approached by an official, Warren Ring. At the insistence of Nick Davis of the BLE he informed me that, unless I changed out of my Reebok gear there and then, I would not be permitted out on to the track.

Nick Davis has always been involved with the BLE since I began. I knew him before, and later he went on to be president. He was always at sports awards or races that I would turn up to in Ireland. I know he has presented me with medals and tried to sweep the dirt under the rug, but I can't accept that what he did that day was an honourable thing.

The hurt of having to strip and change couldn't alter how I felt inside anyway. Deep down I knew that I wasn't ready for this race. I should have stepped off the conveyor belt before it even passed through Atlanta. Those are the worst scenes in my store of career memories – images and feelings so bad that I have banished them from my mind almost completely.

Afterwards people blamed Kim. That was unfair too. It made no difference to Kim. In fact he wanted me to just wear the Asics and be done with it. Most of Kim's business was with Nike anyway. I wanted to wear Reebok because the gear fitted me better than Asics did. I just never liked the cut of the Asics. Nothing more.

I ran that heat, upset and feeling dreadful. I finished and kept my head down. One piece of eye contact with another runner and my secret would be out. I had nothing.

The night after the heat, not for the first time that summer, I woke up in our house in Buckhead to find myself drenched in sweat. I was so cold and so wet that I could wring my T-shirt out and watch the drops fall to the floor in a little puddle. I changed the bedclothes and my T-shirt and went back to bed. I never said a word to anyone.

On the morning of the final itself, Frank and I went for a run, out near the Olympic cycling venue. Frank was the sort of company I needed on the day. My head was spinning with doubts and my body was empty of energy. We hadn't been there long before Frank found himself jogging up and down outside a women's toilet, waiting for me to emerge again. We joked about it and I said I was fine. I am good at that: closing myself off from the world, making people think what I need them to think when it has to be done. It's part of the game of strength. Putting on your game face.

The race was at night. I rested. Ate some rice and fish. We took a drive in the afternoon to kill time. I knew nothing was there in my body but I put the last of my hope in the thought that the Olympic stadium, an excited crowd, the crack of a pistol, those things would startle me back into running on automatic. Just for the most important 15 minutes of my life. That was the bargain with my body. Do this for me and we will get you looked after.

From the start of the race I never felt good that night. We were just playing games with the pace. I'd normally love that, but I felt bad. I hadn't the energy to make any move, and if I did attempt it I couldn't hold on to my position.

Like in the heats, like always or so it seemed, the early running was being done by Sara Wedlund. Some day Sara was going to go away and nobody was going to bother to go after her. In the meantime it was inevitable that she would be caught. People were shifting up and down the gears, not worried about Wedlund, just seeing what they had.

An Olympic final is no time for weakness. By the 1000-metre mark Pauline Konga, a friend of mine from Kenya and a girl I sometimes trained with, was taking us through in 3:06.15. I was hanging in there. Faking it.

About halfway through the race, with six laps to go and after a lot of jostling and shuffling, Pauline Konga still had the lead, but there was an injection of pace and the field was suddenly strung out.

I didn't so much miss the break as look to my body and find myself as I expected to be deep down: heavy-limbed and sluggish and hot. The night wasn't bad, for Atlanta. Not too humid and a bit of a cool breeze. It should have been ideal, but I was sweating huge amounts of fluid.

Suddenly I was trailing the field badly. The gap just opened up further and further over the next lap. At one stage I was vaguely aware of my face large on the huge videotrons, high in the Olympic stadium. A face like death. My secret was out now.

With four laps to go I felt like I was running under the surface in a pool of hot water. I was some 100 metres off the pace, which was still being set by Pauline Konga and Wang Junxia. 100 metres is the difference between being relevant to Pauline and Wang and the feeling of becoming invisible.

I kept going. The Irish voices that had been calling to me in the din were quiet now. I was becoming invisible. I took a lap to think about what I wanted to do. I made a decision. With two laps remaining I came around the back bend and slipped straight out of the stadium down the exit tunnel. Just like that. Race favourite gone. Vanished. 83,000 spectators and a worldwide television audience left to wonder.

I figured, maybe I could save myself and be OK for the 1500 metres. I would leave via the tunnel, escaping the media mixed zone in one neat move. Where the press can't see you. So I disappeared.

Shit. Hadn't thought of this. People in the tunnel. Blazers. I'm upset, and the officials want to bring me to a medical room. I say, 'No. I'm fine.' Then I decided it would be best to get myself together. I stayed a while before I went out and faced people.

I'd walked off the track in the biggest race of my life with the planet watching, and I had no idea what had just happened. I was just saying to myself over and over, 'What did I just do?'

No answers. In the end, the officials led me down to where all the press were anyway.

I just didn't have anything to say. I couldn't say anything. I saw Kim and my family over the railings. With tears streaming down my face, I packed my gear into a small black rucksack, slipped into a white T-shirt and black leggings and just went over to Kim and Mam and Dad. I went over and just asked them what happened. What went wrong?

Gerard was there, too. He hugged me and whispered something supportive. And then somebody led me away again.

Kim and I ran home. Pat Hickey took my gear in the OCI car which had brought me to the stadium. It took 50 minutes for us to run the seven miles to the house in Buckhead, 50 minutes of raw emotion. Kim made me run slowly, talking to me through my tears. He made me talk about what had happened. If I had been on my own, I wouldn't have stopped at the house in Buckhead for long. I would have gone past it and kept going.

Kim talked to me about what I owed myself. He talked about the goodwill that was there for me in the stadium; but what was more important was what I owed. I was the one running more than 100 miles a week, the one doing 400 sit-ups in front of the television in the evening. I was the one busting a gut at the track and in the gym and in the pool and hacking it through all the injuries. He made me look forward instead of back.

By the time we got home, a part of me was already focused on the 1500-metre heats. Versions of the run home that night were published in the next few days which had more to do with the runs. They weren't true. I ran and cried and talked. That was it.

We talked until nearly 4 a.m. I used the will I had used in denying there was something wrong to tell myself now that there was something wrong but that it would be fine in a couple of days.

12

Sunday night. Monday morning.

Before I went to sleep I took a sleeping pill. I usually do after a race, but even sleeping tablets don't do a lot when your body wants to sleep and your head wants to race. I cried some more. All the tension and hurt was draining out of me.

I awoke twice before morning, drenched in sweat again. Woke twice to that freezing cold, 'ice water down the back' reality. I'd run out of an Olympic final. My Olympic final. The world 5000-metre champion who ran off down the tunnel with two laps to go.

I lay there on Monday morning, hoping first that the world would go away and then realizing that the previous 24 hours were probably going to divide my life in two. I would think of things forever as having happened before Atlanta or after Atlanta.

When I got up, people were gathered as if there had been a death. Pat Hickey came out to the house. Paying his respects and asking what the plan of action was. I was stubborn about wanting to carry on as normal. I went out for a 25-minute run so that I could pull my thoughts in. I was feeling every step with my body, waiting for myself to feel bad. It was OK. Two days to the 1500-metre heats. Who knows? Lazarus must have had his doubtful moments too.

The Olympic Council felt that a press conference was needed. Word about Friday night's gear fiasco with Nick Davis had also got out. There was a lot of talking to be done. I didn't want to be part of a two-pronged press conference so I said I would do my bit first and then they could go with the gear war. Or vice versa. Whichever pleased them. I agreed to do the press conference because I felt that I had to try to explain myself. I thought maybe I would also have answers for myself.

People wanted me to see a doctor. At the same time they knew that they were wasting their time. The 1500 metres was what was keeping me putting one foot in front of the other. A doctor would do what doctors do. He would be cautious.

I declined to do anything more than speak to the Olympic team medic, Dr Joe Cummisky, about what the problem was. I knew Joe Cummisky and always found him so meticulous. That Monday in Atlanta, that meticulous nature scared me. I wanted a clean bill of health even if it had to be counterfeit and forged.

I knew Joe Cummisky would find something wrong with me if he examined me properly because, well, there was probably something quite wrong with me. And when he found it he wasn't going to let me run the 1500 because if he did he could end up as a professional laughing stock. And being kept back for medical reasons was not how I wanted to not win the 1500. If it was going to end, I wanted it to be on the track. The rest of my life would be for regrets and 'what ifs'.

They had a press conference in the afternoon. I went because it was a way of thanking people. And a way of giving some explanation. I had to explain why Sunday wasn't such a great day and leave people with the idea that there were some great days around the corner with the 1500 metres.

The press conference got out of hand. Soon I was answering questions about my bowel movements and what the Olympic Council had in a press release called the Big D. Those were the highlights. Apparently.

To be honest, I don't really remember the press conference too well. I was in a trance by then. I couldn't tell you in any detail where the conference was held or what I was wearing or who was there. I think I have done a good job in eliminating it all from my memory.

In the years afterwards I think I refused to talk about Atlanta for such a long time that in the end I really didn't know anything for certain about it. Atlanta had turned into a bad and surreal experience. The broiling humidity. My body betraying me. Being made to strip before a race. Sitting there in that immense, ugly building, looking at the Irish media and talking to them about diarrhoea. This was to be my Olympics? My time!

And of course when the questions for me were over and done with, the press conference segued into the gear issue and nobody excused me or made any allowance for a little break or recess. So I sat there through the details of my humiliation the previous Friday, saying only that perhaps 'humiliation' was a little too strong a term to use.

I sat there, filling up with despair and anger and starting to shiver. The air conditioning was on cold. We had come into this immense Inforum Building where the press conference was being held and the heat outside was sufficient to cook a chicken in. Now it was freezing in here. And I was miserable.

When it was over I went for lunch with my parents and was relieved to have normal company. We talked about the 1500 metres. I was confident in that way you have to be to your parents when you know they are concerned. They were just being parents, Mam and Dad. Wanting to look after me. Getting around Atlanta in public transport, sightseeing at a Games where their daughter was one of the bad-news stories.

After the race the previous night they had dutifully gone to a party in the Irish House, out at Decatur. The Irish House was sort of an unofficial headquarters/pub for the Irish at the Games. Everyone had planned to be celebrating a track gold medal. Instead it was a wake, but Mam and Dad went because they felt that an O'Sullivan face should be shown there. People were polite and subdued. Then Mam and Dad caught the train home.

I think I nearly pulled it off for the 1500 metres. I nearly fooled myself into thinking that I was OK. Frank came with me to the warm-up track because, well, because he is Frank. He knew me well. He knew that, having had a problem, I would be over-analysing how I was feeling. If I got worried or scared, I would get lonely. He was there to look after me. One of my big brothers.

At the warm-up track, we saw Michael Johnson, the American sprinter, getting ready. He was so focused-looking, he would have stuck with his routine if there had been an earthquake and a small war at the warm-up track. Frank and I agreed that he had his game face on. He was a good example for me to see. In 1992 he had famously eaten some spicy sausage and got food poisoning, weeks before the Games. Like myself, he had kept his mouth shut as he lost pound after pound and felt his strength ebbing away. He thought he could master his body until the moment he put it on the line down on the track.

So as Michael Johnson had his game face on, I promised Frank I would put mine on too. I wasn't feeling good inside but the effort of convincing Frank that I was fine and dandy helped me fool myself as well. I got the last-call sign and left Frank behind. By then I had convinced myself that I was going to qualify and buy myself just a little more time before the final.

This time it was hot out there. I hated that stadium, with its black interior and the feeling that you were in a pot or a cauldron. The little bit of conviction I had mustered up died in the heat down there. I came in tenth out of eleven. It was the Olympics and a time to be merciless. The girls, runners whom I had bossed and maybe intimidated for years, saw my lather of sweat and my fatigue. They saw the tension all over my face. They ate me alive. Just as I would have done to them.

I finished 21 seconds slower than my personal best time. Out of the 1500 metres. Out of the Olympic Games. I left the stadium without saying a word. There was nothing that could be said to me. No next race to dangle in front of me. It was all over bar the sobbing.

I know I went back to the stadium that evening, the night of my last race in Atlanta. I don't know why. When I got there, I felt as if I didn't belong, as if I was trespassing. The Games had nothing to do with me any more. I scarcely remember a single thing about it: the heat, the blackness. Putting down time. I can't recall how I got back there, the races I watched, anything about the whole thing.

For the 1500-metre final I went along with Frank. He was working for RTE. He would park the car in one of those front yards that were all around the stadium, places where kids would take a few dollars to park the car.

I just trailed after Frank and commentated on the 1500 final. I think because Frank is so light-hearted and talkative and good-natured, he was just trying to make me do things and keep me going. 'You have to come out of this and walk again,' he'd tell me. He just included me in what he was doing. I wanted to go off by myself, but it would have been too dark a place I would have gone to.

I don't remember leaving Atlanta. The closing ceremony was on 4 August. My diary says I was in London by then.

13

After Atlanta I suppose I was a bit more distant from the world. Distant in a different way from before. If people felt I was stand-offish previously, now I felt isolated. I just felt removed from life.

I cried myself to sleep every night for two weeks. I knew it was only a race and I knew the world had moved on, but it was a race which had defined me, how I felt and how I was perceived. I had kept myself so locked down and controlled for so long. Now everything went. I wanted to hide from everyone. I wanted to see nobody. Occasionally I would have to spend time with people. I would pump myself up to be as pleasant and cheery as possible. I couldn't accept pity or sympathy.

Then there were all these letters coming in. I would go to Kim's office in Hampton Hill. He had a green-and-white striped couch in there and his desk was off to the side; and I would sit on this couch, reading these letters and just finding myself crying. The way people wrote would touch me. I still have big boxes and bags of these letters in the basement of the house in London. I used to write back, take a bunch of letters home with me, bring autograph cards and send them back. There was so much post it was unbelievable.

I suppose it was good to read those letters, a little like therapy. People would say positive things about me, and I needed to read and hear positive things about myself. I devoured the letters, loved the ones that came to me from little kids with pictures attached that they had drawn themselves. I badly needed to feel a connection with people. I would write back and feel like I was doing something productive. When I got back to training eventually, I had to tear myself away from the mountain of letters and get back to work, but Irish people are good letter-writers.

I loved and appreciated that contact. In the rest of my life I felt so alone. At the time I had built up this image of strength, put a wall around myself that protected me. I had felt as if I was in control of everything; I only put myself into situations where I was in control. Then in Atlanta it unravelled in this most public way and the wall came tumbling down. All of us have a face that we show to the world; suddenly, when everyone sees that you aren't as strong as you thought you were, when they see you stripped down and broken, you become so vulnerable that every-thing affects you more. All your armour is gone. The way you would run the opposite way on the track during warm-ups. The battle face you would wear in races, no matter how bad you were feeling. The reputation for working longer and harder than anybody else. When it came to the big stage, the one that mattered, you slipped out through the back door in tears. Everything is taken away from you after that.

You start to wonder what you will do next, how you will put one foot in front of the other and start again. How people see you and define you. Has that changed too? Has it changed in the same way that you see yourself and define yourself? Or worse? How will you feel, the next time you step out on to a warm-up track, everyone looking and whispering. Will there even be a next time?

What hurt? In the days between disasters and in the days afterwards I was stuck in Atlanta, with the Olympics unfolding all around me. Life went on for everybody. Events ran on time. Medals were presented and anthems were played and people gath-ered in stadiums or around televisions to watch it all. And I was just standing still, trying to find answers. But in the immediate aftermath at least there were distractions.

In the Irish Olympic offices all the papers and the faxes sent from home would come in. I wouldn't read them. I would catch a few headlines and know the flavour, but generally I didn't know what was said in Ireland. I didn't want to know. On the one hand, I knew there was a lot of sympathy and goodwill at home; on the other hand, I was hurt.

So what hurt, apart from the obvious failure to achieve

something I had set out to achieve from a long way out? It hurt that I had crashed through the warning signs so recklessly myself. As a kid back in Cobh I remember days when I would be cold and shivering with the flu and I would pull myself together at the front gate and show a different face inside the house so that there would be no issue about me going out for a run. At night I would cough into my pillow, stifling all the noise so that I could run to school in the morning. I tried to do that as well for Atlanta. I would feel bad in those sessions and gather myself and tell myself that I wasn't allowed to feel bad, that it was weakness. I would plough on harder, running myself down more.

I look back at my diaries on the run-in to Atlanta and they are full of those alarm-sign entries like 'felt bad', 'felt really bad', 'felt a bit better than yesterday'. But the diaries are still full of other entries. There is no space of a week or two when I might have stepped away and refuelled myself. I was convinced that the harder I worked and the more I put myself through, the more inevitable the reward would be.

It hurt to get it so wrong. It hurt to have been so self-reliant, and for my own instincts to be wrong. Frank and Marcus always said I was headstrong and I never took that altogether as an insult.

Then there was the isolation that comes with failure.

I don't think it was what people said. I was more hurt by the simple thought that I had let everyone down. Little things like the flag incident in Gothenburg the year before had taught me something about the connection between myself and home. I wanted it to be right in Atlanta, for everybody just to enjoy it. I suppose too I felt that some people were glad to see me fail. I knew that some people thought I had it coming to me. I had been brought down a few pegs.

Although there was a lot of unpleasantness, there were good things too, people who cared about me when I was down. Some days in Atlanta I would go out to lunch with my parents; they were around the house, fussing, worried and naturally concerned. I was so numb. I had nothing to say. Mam and Dad had stayed in a separate house and organized everything themselves for the

Olympics, so it was hard for them. They did all the things at the Olympics that you don't do if you are an athlete: went to see things and places. There was the experience of the whole thing there for them . . . and their daughter disintegrating at the same time. Seeing them coming and going and taking time out to worry over me made it all seem even more sad.

I've talked about my difficulties with the BLE, but it would be wrong of me to tar everyone with the same brush. The medical team, Brendan O'Brien, Siobhain Treacy and Marie-Elaine Grant, were great. I always knew they were there for me. Throughout my career the medical people were really good. And generally the coaches were too, and the team management, people like Sean Naughton, real athletics people. They have the instinct to put an arm around you like they would for any kid who had just lost a race. They feel for you. I think they felt they had more of a role when I was down. They don't want to be fussing about you when you are going well. In Atlanta and afterwards I needed them and they were there, and I will always be grateful.

I never read much about the Atlanta Olympics afterwards. I decided at the time that I didn't ever want to watch the race again. I buried the whole experience in a capsule. Occasionally some part of it would leak out into my brain, but I locked it away. I was surprised 11 years later to sit down to watch a DVD of '20 Moments That Shook Irish Sport' to see those days on the screen for the first time. I was surprised that they made me cry yet again. There is something still raw about it. Years and years on, I still know the truth of what my dad said: nobody died. It still makes me emotional, though.

I often wonder now what sort of person I would have become if it had worked out as I'd hoped. I think if Sydney had given me gold, it would have cancelled out Atlanta completely. If I had done that, then Athens would not have been so final. What happens to you at an Olympic Games has a sort of domino effect on the rest of your life. In Sydney I was happy to have got a medal; but to have been beaten by such a small margin, it made a little space in the back of my head. If I could go back and change things, I would go back and change Sydney rather than Atlanta – but that is just using Sydney as a device to wipe out Atlanta, I suppose.

There was lots of stuff comparing Kim with Erik de Bruin. On one level Kim knew what was going on, but he was never really tuned in to it. For me it had always been, 'OK, what's next?' And for Kim that was still the case. It was on to the next thing for Kim. Go back out and race again. Racing will make it better.

For Kim, if you were running fast, then where the race was or what it was didn't even matter. It was a race and you were going well. That was what feeling good was all about. So his idea was that I should get back out and race as soon as I could. Stupidly, I tagged along to Zurich and Cologne but didn't compete there, and more stupidly I ended up going to a race in Rieti.

There was just enough residual fitness left in me to win a race over 3000 metres. At the time that distance didn't stretch me. A 5000 would have told me where I was at. A 3000-metre race is over so quickly you can escape anything with that fitness. The first kilometre was over real quick, I hung around for a little, and next thing I knew, it was near the end and time to do a bit of work. I won. Everyone said I was back. People were saying it, so I believed it because I really wanted to believe it.

Rieti painted a false picture for me, and I allowed myself to think that I could go on and run in the Grand Prix finals in Milan. Maybe I'd feel bad and win again, stretch my sequence of Grand Prix wins. I had won in Rieti, so Kim couldn't believe that I wouldn't be able to do the same in Milan.

And I tried to believe right along with him. Perhaps that would be the secret. Just keep going and come out the other side.

Kim was oblivious anyway. Back on a high. At the time, he had Daniel Komen, the great Kenyan runner, under his wing. For various reasons Daniel hadn't gone to the Olympics. At the time, he was back in London, training, and now he was out breaking world records. Kim was full of this. The speed, the purity of just going as fast as you could go. It was a drug for Kim.

I couldn't tell him that I just didn't care any more. I hadn't the heart for the obsession we had shared. I couldn't sit him down and say, 'Kim, I don't need to talk about running right now.' In a way I should have done what I did in 1997. I should have just stopped and said, 'Let's not try again for a long time,' but I was out there every day in Bushy Park, trying to get a fast lap of the park, trying to get under 40 minutes so that I could convince myself and convince Kim that I was OK.

It just wasn't working, but I still thought it would. You never give up. You keep thinking it will work. Do the things you did before, and they will work again. Do them harder. More often. I worked harder after the Chinese came to Stuttgart. And I had two good years. Maybe the same thing would happen for me now. I'd come out stronger.

This time it was different, though. I wasn't lonely after Stuttgart; it finished on an encouraging note for me: a silver medal. Now I just wanted to stop, but I hadn't the courage to tell Kim. I hadn't the heart even to tell myself. Suppose I stopped and never started running again. There seemed to be no way of picking up the threads of life again if not through running.

I suppose now, years later, when I have the wisdom to step back, I know. After you have done it once, you know. In 1997, when I ran in Athens and it didn't work out, I knew straight away I wasn't going to run any more races. It is embarrassing and humiliating to go out and try to win races that you know you could win if you were all right but that you can't win because you are in trouble.

Physically and mentally you just can't do it, but you put yourself through the whole process of getting ready, doing it all, convincing yourself, step by step, all the way to the race that you can conquer this and that by winning you will feel better again. When you are all alone on the line though, you don't believe in your heart that you can do it. You are lost before you take the first step. You might as well stop, but you have set it all in motion. So you say to yourself, if I don't try how will I know? You do know already, though.

In 1997, in Turin at the World Cross Country and in Athens at the World Championships, I knew before I stood on the start line that it wasn't there for me. It wasn't in my heart or in my legs. There was something missing, something not clicking that normally allows you to do what you can do. It's like your focus is taken away. You feel really weak. No belief. You are all over the place. You have no determination or sticking power, no ability to stick like glue, no matter what. It all comes apart. I still have no real idea how or why that happens. It happens to loads of people in different walks of life, I suppose, but when you are the thing that you do, it is the loneliest place in the world.

And it was a desperately lonely time. Not just 1996 and its aftermath, but even before that. I ran and ran and kept going, but generally I was so lonely. Whenever I stopped and stood still I felt that loneliness. So I trained myself never to stop.

Probably from the time when I decided not to spend so much of the year in America, instead spending more time in London, I lost the social side of life at the end of the year. I ran through the season, racing almost non-stop. I'd have a break at the end of summer and then start straight back into it again. The breaks were never breaks for me, even though nothing was going to happen between times. I still lived running. 24/7. So did Kim.

I knew inside that I was young and living in London. I had some money, I could do more if I'd had somebody to do it with. Kim was the ABC as I called it then: Agent. Boyfriend. Coach. When we weren't racing we were planning to be racing. I would be there reading *Athletics Weekly*, magazines and books about running. There was no Internet or I would have been reading that constantly too, scouring it for times and races.

It was lonely. So lonely. The highlight of my Christmas Day was when I went for a run in London. I just cooked myself dinner and that was it. Kim was there, he would come over and then go off wherever. His big thing was always to work on Christmas Day. He was always determined never to take a day off. Generally he would fly somewhere on Christmas Day. He had a daughter in New York. He would fly somewhere long haul on Christmas Day because it was easy. He hated people on the plane offering him Christmas cake. Just wasn't his scene.

At the same time, when I was winning I could see why I was doing it and could measure the sacrifices that I made against some end goal. I believed it would be worth it. In defeat that was all gone. People would say, 'So you lost a race or two, there will be more races.' For me, though, where I was at that time and for a long time before that, winning races was how I defined myself. Running defined me. Always had. Winning races, being tough, being able for anything.

You could beat me for a while; but when I figured out how to beat you, I would keep on beating you. After Barcelona I entered races to pick off those who had beaten me. After the 3000 in Stuttgart I came back in the 1500. After 1993 I put together 1994 and 1995 and ended up as World Champion. Now I had fallen apart.

There were a million rumours. All false. All circulating. I had been pregnant. I had caught Kim in bed with somebody. I had miscarried. Kim had caught me in bed with somebody. On the famous run home from the stadium I had stopped to empty my bowels seven or eight times. All these stories floated around like a cloud above my head. All the comparisons between my failure and Michelle Smith's success. All the judgements that I wasn't able to handle big occasions. In some quarters I went from being the girl who never saw a race that she didn't want to win to being the girl who never saw a big race that didn't scare her.

I was never so low that I wanted to harm myself, but I did want to walk away. I wanted to hide. I went for tests in Limerick. Essentially, they said that I was run down and fatigued, my batteries were completely flat, that I had picked up a urinary tract infection. The simplicity of the diagnosis was frustrating.

I had to focus on life just to keep going. No matter how low I felt, no matter how much time I'd spent crying, I'd go out. I'd see people, I'd say hello, I'd feel great for those few seconds. I'd come back in and feel that those few greetings had passed for company. Then I'd go out and run again in the evenings.

On the one hand, I hated running. On the other, I just wished I could keep running forever. Coming home after a run, shutting the door, being alone with my thoughts: I hated it. I did things in slow motion. There was no rush to go anywhere. I moved around as if I were underwater. I experienced the world in that same muffled way.

I was friendly with Alison Wyeth, the runner from England. Alison lived in Isleworth, some three or four miles away. We'd meet for a run once a week, for some circuits every Monday. That was the highlight of my week, every week. I lived for my runs with Alison.

Most of the runs I did, I did all by myself. I came home and wrote what I did every day into my diary and I would say to myself, I did it. It was like homework. A duty. It had to be done. I had to write it down. At the end I would have a full calendar, a series of boxes full of training sessions, and I could look at it and tell myself I was happy. I had done that. It would convert into something that would make me happy. Surely it would.

I wasn't happy, but I was able to rationalize it and tell myself this is what I have to do. This is what I do. This is what I am.

Before Atlanta I didn't really feel alone because I was working towards something. After Atlanta I felt, what was it all for? Why do I do all this? The ultimate thing you want to achieve you don't get. Are people laughing at you? Should you start all over again? Maybe walk away? After Atlanta I was starting all over again without the nerve or the optimism.

One thing I did, later on in 1996, was an RTE television interview. It had a big effect on me. It wasn't the greatest interview or show in the world, just a way of explaining what had happened and thanking a lot of people for their support. For me it was something else, too.

It was so good, though, having the television people over at the time. Nobody has any idea how much I wanted their company, the noise of them around the place. The sound of them laughing and talking. Bill O'Herlihy, the presenter, and George Hamilton, the commentator, came over from Dublin. They were all around the house. Lights and cables and microphones and guys doing the sound. They were tiptoeing at first because they thought it was sensitive and I was moody. It was good to talk about it. I wished they would never go away. I loved making tea for them and helping set things up. I just needed the company badly. It was great to have people come and watch me training and to hear them saying things that suggested that they believed that it wasn't the end for me. They assumed (or let on to assume) that I would be back just as strong as ever. They had great hope for me and wanted to put that hope into the programme. That actually took away a big chunk of the loneliness.

I took their company and the way they saw me still and I made something of it. That small thing, talking about it to them in front of cameras, made me believe that I could look back and accept everything and not be too bothered and upset. I could put the disappointment into a box and move on.

If other people had hope for me and belief in me, I could get on with life.

14

For a while people did nothing but ask what had been wrong with me and how was I feeling. The explanation that I carried around, that I had had an infection and had been generally run down, seemed too ordinary to have been at the root of such a failure. I went with half the theories myself. There had to be something bigger.

A friend told me that mercury fillings took your energy away. I went and had all mine out. I saw other doctors, had more tests. Till eventually I gave up and decided to move on. Nobody was going to come up with a huge, previously overlooked reason that would explain it all to me. I had done too much and not taken care of myself. I had crashed through all the warning signs. That was it and that was all. Looking back wasn't helping me get through it all.

To kill time, some days I'd drift into Kim's office. I actually did some accounting work there, just to fill my time and give myself something to do. I got really bored though, and I was making other people uncomfortable. I decided I might as well be out running or going to the gym.

I noticed that, when I was in the office, if Kim wasn't there the atmosphere was so much better. As soon as Kim came in, it was like everyone was scared. We all had to be hard at work. We weren't to talk. He was a very authoritarian figure, very driven. He was the boss and everyone else was doing the work. He didn't believe in playtime. The only playtime was training and racing.

Kim wasn't a demonstrative man. He didn't understand or want to understand complex emotions. He would never say that he was disappointed in me or that he blamed me for failing in Atlanta. He just moved on and expected me to do the same, but things just stopped moving on between us. A gap which we had never noticed before opened up between us after Atlanta. The tension just increased because things weren't going forward as they had been beforehand. I couldn't help feeling that if we were all going to move on, it was time for a change.

There had been a lot of pressure in general around the place in the lead-up to Atlanta. In the time we had been together I had changed. I had become more willing to stand up to Kim, more willing to challenge him about things relating to training. In the sessions when things weren't going right I would pull out and argue with him, whereas once I would have tried to work through it regardless. In the seasons before, I had been more submissive; I would accept anything. If Kim said, 'Do this,' I would do it. X session? OK. Y session. Good!

Now it was different. If I said, 'I can't really do this today,' Kim would ask why not. We would argue. After Atlanta we started arguing over races. Sometimes I would throw in the towel. I remember a 2000-metre race in Sheffield. I just threw in the towel. And we argued. He said, 'Don't ever do that again.' I thought, I will if I want to.

Things like that would get me fired up. I was looking for the chance to say, 'I know I can do that on my own. Let me do it on my own.' I was looking to have a say in things. You question a lot of things as you get older anyway. I wasn't the starry-eyed kid from Cobh who had gone to a meeting in Crystal Palace and rubbernecked all the stars any more. I just felt the need for me to be more in control of what I was doing.

The thing with a coach is, you have to have faith in everything. If you are going to work that hard, there is no room for questions. If Atlanta had brought two gold medals, maybe all the questions would have gone away. As things were, I had started doubting it all, doubting myself and then, by extension, Kim. I didn't question things too much before, but I was growing older, life was changing me and I was just becoming more my own person. I wanted to do things. I wanted to be in charge. In the void after Atlanta I had all the chances I wanted to do that.

Looking back, perhaps I could see it coming. If I had been more willing to stand up to Kim and said that things needed to slow down, maybe Atlanta would have been different; but then again I think we both shared the same madness at the time. Arguing with Kim was one thing. Stepping back for a few weeks to get myself right was another.

After Atlanta I wasn't sure what to do. The Olympic Games had been such a big story back home and, although some newspapers decided to blame Kim for a lot of what happened, that was unfair. I didn't want us to end up with it looking as if I had sacked Kim and for it to turn into a mini-version of the sort of fuss that would follow the sacking of an Irish soccer manager.

I was too confused about it all to do anything like make an announcement anyway. My life and career revolved around Teddington and the community of athletes whom Kim was responsible for. I wanted change but I didn't want to walk away from all that.

I didn't want to draw anything on myself. No more fuss. I moved along, slipping from one thing to another, avoiding Kim. I had been entered in a whole list of races after Atlanta and didn't want to run in any of them. Kim would be calling me, leaving messages, asking me what I wanted to do. I would ignore him completely. He would cancel my entry at the last minute.

In September, foolishly, I went to Milan, thinking I would compete in the Grand Prix final there. I had been training without enthusiasm since I came home from Atlanta in early August and, having fooled myself with a win in Rieti, I decided that I would go to Milan.

The night was a disaster. I was in bad form. Paula Radcliffe was out ahead of me in the first two laps and I just tried to focus on the number on Paula's back and to stay with her. I found that I literally couldn't even do that. My head was everywhere except in the race. I wasn't there mentally, and when I checked I wasn't there physically either. So I just walked off the track and sat down. It was a small enough disaster. In terms of pain it hardly registered when compared to Atlanta. I had wanted to know. I had gone to Milan and found out the hard way. I could just write it off to experience.

In October I told Kim the bad news. Not that he hadn't figured it out for himself by then. I wrote him a long letter. I walked over to him and told him that I knew I wouldn't have been able to tell him face to face everything that was in the letter, that I wouldn't have been able to get through it all. So I'd had to write it down. There it was, all in an envelope on small pages – six of them. Six pages sifting through all the details of an ending.

I'm not very good at talking but not too bad at writing. I do good emails. If somebody asks me a question, I can get it all out on an email better than in speech. Kim understood, I think.

Anyway, we never talked about it again. Kim was like that. No questions. No mulling. No analysis. It was never mentioned. From being the ABC he went back to being just the A, my agent. An agent whose client didn't really talk to him because she was so messed up in the head. What he thought about it all I never really knew. He didn't do emotions much. Kim just accepted it and moved on. Always moving on.

I went away and coached myself for quite a while. I did all the same things but I didn't have somebody watching me and expecting things of me. I was happy and miserable at the same time. After I went to Limerick for the post-Olympic tests I had promised myself, I started doing some serious training – but not trying to run as far as I could or as fast as I could. I decided to head back to America in November, just in time for Thanksgiving and my birthday, both on the same day. I needed the company and the friendships I had there. I told myself that I would have all year to get fast. I just needed some solid steady runs and a happy heart for the time being.

In London, before I headed back, I ran for three weeks with Alan Storey's group, and there were two benefits. It was great just to meet up with people and be normal. They were so welcoming and unassuming that it gave me a huge boost. Alan, whom Kim had introduced me to, is a great coach. He has a different view of life and training from myself and from anyone else I had been exposed to.

'Sonia, you don't have to do everything eyeballs out,' he would tell me as he tried to explain patiently that there would be a time for running fast and a time for just maintaining.

So there were the friendships and a new voice. Plus I could also see the improvement in myself each week. We did a road circuit, which was a bit of a shock to the system, and then a track session where I felt awkward and uncoordinated until about halfway through the session, and then a hilly road loop (at Wimbledon), where I felt a lot more involved in the session. I even surprised myself that I could run well and enjoy a hilly session.

There was a reason for every run that I did from then on: mostly collecting oxygen so that I would have lots of it to spare when I needed it most at the end of races. Everything is different. I have heart rate guidelines now to think about while training. Less than 165 beats per minute for long runs, even slower for recovery-type runs. 175–180 b.p.m. for tempo runs like a lap of Bushy Park. And a rate of 180–185 for interval sessions.

In London, things had been encouraging. I had managed to do 39:07 on my third week back, doing the park lap, and I wasn't killing myself either.

Before coming to Philly I did a lot of recovery runs down along the river, through Hampton Court. These easy runs had been great for me. I'd run a lot by myself and really had time to think extensively about my feelings and beliefs and my plans for the future. I came to believe that I had to be happy about what I was doing from now on. I must be in control of my training and what I really wanted to achieve in life. And for a while everything fell into place. I began dreaming again of great things every day. And there was a voice telling me that the dreams could come true if I worked hard. But sensibly!

Being back in Haverford was good. On the day after I arrived I ran the jet lag out of my legs with a run up at Valley Green with Marcus and Gerry O'Reilly and had a massage afterwards. I was still tired from the trip, but the next day I did a morning run and an afternoon run. Both of them were good. In the afternoon I did some training circuits at the local Y.

On my birthday (28 November) I went to Fairmount Park with

Brendan Mahon (a brother of my old boyfriend Terrence) for a 5-mile Turkey Trot. Did 25:49 and felt pretty good. In fact I sprinted the last 200 metres and won the whole race. OK, it was a Thanksgiving Day Turkey Trot in Fairmount Park, but it felt good! The biggest step in my rehabilitation so far: winning a Thanksgiving Day Turkey Trot!

Although things were coming together there were still little fragments of the past in my system. I found that, no matter how much work I do, I have trouble sleeping at night. Just thinking too much.

And too much to think about!

15

I know it's corny, but I really don't remember when I met Nic Bideau first. Apparently I sat on a plane right next to him going to Nice in 1993 or 1994. I don't recall our conversation, though Nic is sure that we spoke, especially as he recounts a funny incident on the the plane while I was sitting next to him. As I had just won a few races and set some Irish records, I picked up the Irish papers to read the reports and see if any pictures had got into the paper from my recent races. Frank O'Mara had been reading the papers and when they were passed back to me he had taken out all the athletics and pictures, so, as you can imagine, I was puzzled why there were no stories in the papers.

The first time I really met Nic properly was in 1995 when I went to Australia for a training camp. At that time Nic was a journalist writing for the *Herald Sun*. He was organizing the taking of a picture with myself and all the Kenyans whom Kim had brought along to Melbourne. Nic said he would do something separate with me. He organized a cameraman to take a picture of me at some nice waterfall in Melbourne.

In 1995 Cathy Freeman was just getting famous in Australia and athletics was beginning to take off there. The Aussies were already building up at that stage for their Olympic Games. Cathy Freeman was going to be a star. And this guy, the journalist Nic Bideau, he was Cathy's fella.

At that time it was hard to be in Australia and not know the story of Cathy Freeman and Nic. At the age of 16, Cathy had won gold in the 4 x 100-metre relay at the 1990 Commonwealth Games in Auckland. She had gone on to Barcelona in 1992, where she became the first Aboriginal track-and-field athlete to represent Australia at an Olympic Games. In 1994 she went on to win the 200 metres and 400 metres at the Commonwealth Games in

Victoria, Canada, where she had draped herself symbolically in the Aboriginal and Australian flags. Nic had been a sports journalist when he first met Cathy in Sydney in late 1989. She was young and unknown and was going for trials for the following Auckland Commonwealth Games. Nic was 29; Cathy was 16. He took her under his wing, giving her guidance and advice, and he became her manager. By 1991 they were living together. (The parallels with myself and Kim were obvious; but in athletics, where an obsession is shared that way, relationships like that are quite commonplace.)

Anyway, 1995 was my first occasion to do any serious training in Australia. Kim had brought a whole crew of us down: the big bunch of Kenyans plus Peter Elliott, John Mayock, Bob Kennedy and Steve Holman. They all came out. The Tan was the area in Melbourne where we ran. I know now that Melbourne is full of great places to run, but back then we did all our running there. Kim needed to know where we were and whether we were doing four laps of the Tan or six of Fawkner Park next door. He needed to know we weren't just running aimlessly around the woods, getting lost. So we ran on the Tan every day.

I ran with Nic sometimes. He'd had a weight dropped on his foot in the gym and was just getting back to doing some running. I would be running and I would meet Nic. He would turn around and run with me. I would never slow down. Just amusing myself.

The whole Australian thing became like a schools exchange programme. Not long after we had left Australia, the Australians we had known there followed us back to London. We helped Nic to buy a house for his training group in Hampton Hill. At that stage I would meet Nic and usually a few others every day for a run around Bushy Park. He was just one of a whole slew of Aussies who seemed to materialize in our lives at that time: Peter Jess, Nic's friend and business partner, and Cathy Freeman and Nic and a raggle-taggle bunch of hangers-on and other athletes.

Amazingly, the house they bought in London back then is still an athletics house. Craig Mottram now owns it. He bought our old house in Australia too. (Craig is unbelievable. He had a nice apartment in Oz, but moved from that to buy our house. He had a small apartment in London and decided it was too small, so he bought Nic's original place in London. We now live in Hampton Court; he is in Hampton Hill, just by another gate of the park. If he runs near our house I shudder lest he decides to pop in and offer to buy it!)

So I knew Nic for quite a while and, towards the end of 1996 when they had all gone back to Australia, I began to spend time talking to him in addition to meeting for runs. He would call me on the phone sometimes. I wasn't feeling up for running. He was trying to make me feel good, to convince me that I was all right. His big thing was for me to come to Australia any time. No problem. They would look after me.

I'm not sure what connection we had made, but for some reason when Nic started calling me on the phone I was grateful that somebody, anybody, was taking an interest. I remember talking to him on the phone one day and he was telling me to relax and to go out there and take it easy, but to come back, to be great again; and I was saying yes, yes, yes, and I was eating a huge bar of chocolate at the time. He was saying, 'You are a good athlete. Take your time and get back into it,' and I was saying in my head, I'm useless, never will be anything but useless so I'm going to take my time and eat all this chocolate and then have more.

It all helped, though!

Apart from the phone calls and the emails I didn't actually see Nic until I went to Hawaii for a mile race in December 1996.

On 3 December, a Tuesday, I travelled to Honolulu. The first two days there were easy going. Some runs in the heat, a photo session with the *Running Times*, dinner at the country club with some Nike types. Nic was coming down to Hawaii for a Nike conference. We had arranged to meet there. I think both of us knew by then what would happen. I was happy. Ran well. Won a race. My diary for the night of Thursday, 5 December, finishes with the words, 'can't wait'.

And as for Friday the 6th, it begins as follows: 'Nick gets in at past midnight . . . very special moments, I will never forget!

Same loop as previously . . . bit tired but OK once we got going w/Nicholas. Good to run with Nic again.'

And that's how it was. In recovering from Atlanta, Honolulu and Nic played a huge part. I raced on the Saturday. I won and felt good, really good again. I felt like myself. We ate that night at Planet Hollywood and I ran with Nic the next couple of days. On the following Wednesday I travelled through the night to Sydney and on to Melbourne. Still chasing the warm weather. Still trying to find what I was looking for, but with a good idea that I knew that I was close to both.

I got back to Melbourne a few days ahead of Nic. The wait for him to arrive home in the city was long but not too stressful: running through the Tan, the odd movie, keeping myself distracted.

Nic got back on the Saturday after I had arrived in Melbourne. He came to the house, was back all of ten minutes, and the two of us set off for the beach. Away from questions, away from the real world. Just to a quiet and peaceful spot with fresh air and good trails, hills and great company. The sooner people around us accept and understand us, the better it will be for Nic and the less he will be looking over his shoulder. Getting away was the best thing we could have done.

The weekend was just talking and running. Nic is a strong runner and he beats me on the steps and the hills. On Monday, after a run on the beach we headed back to Melbourne. I could feel Nic getting more tense as we got nearer the city.

Apparently he and Cathy weren't seeing each other very much. They were all finished and in the process of starting a bit of a war, sorting things out, they hoped, but not getting anywhere. Nic said that he and Cathy had been together for a purpose for a couple of years and had since grown apart, but he had to keep it together because he was coaching her and managing her and everything else on the way to Atlanta.

It's not a love story we are writing here, but I had known the doors were open. We had been talking a lot and had written a few emails. We were considering the next step, definitely. (Later, in a book, Cathy claimed to have seen one of these emails and she said that what appeared on the screen made her 'physically sick. It was virtually a love letter.' This was a bit exaggerated.) We did write a lot to each other in emails and there were numerous phone calls when Nic was trying both to be supportive towards me in general and to get me to move forward after Atlanta. This would have been October, well past the Olympics, and I still hadn't cleared my mind of the disaster in Atlanta. When I spoke to Nic and emailed him, he was always telling me about how desperate his own situation with Cathy was getting. I suppose, like me, he felt like he was in deep with her training and management and he didn't want to let her hang out to dry just after he had got her to winning Olympic silver in Atlanta. He told me that they had plenty of rows and so on and were not moving forward as a couple. In a way we were supporting each other, listening to each other, and eventually we made a connection so that, even though thousands of miles away, we made each other feel good and positive about ourselves so we could go about our daily lives happy and relaxed because we each had someone who cared about us more than the other person we each had in our lives – that is, Kim or Cathy.

That autumn Cathy had moved out of the house she and Nic had shared in Stanley Street. There has been lots of sad tabloid stuff ever since about various things that are supposed to have happened, like Cathy rooting in a dustbin for condoms or signs of an affair or arriving at the house at dawn, hoping to confront myself and Nic, and cutting her wrist after smashing a mirror in anger and then smearing the walls with blood! I never saw any of the breaking glass or the fights, but I saw the remnants that Nic missed when he was cleaning up. Then again, I had David Matthews around down there, so we would just laugh it off and say she must be mad! Better stay clear of her!

David had also come to Melbourne and was staying in Stanley Street too. We never discussed matters a whole lot, but he knew what was going on and he was fantastic at distracting me from lots of things that could easily have rocked my boat or upset the apple cart. We did all our runs together, circuit training every second day, and David was always great for a laugh to ease the tension that could creep into the house. Nic never told me everything about what went on with Cathy or about how everyone would call him up to give him a piece of their mind; but I didn't really want to know either. As far as I was concerned, his personal life with Cathy was over, and as long as I could block her out of my mind, then I could get on with everything that was important to me ... blocking things out seems to be my solution to all problems!!

(By the way, there was only one time when Cathy and I came face to face. It was when she was really angry in Oslo in 1998, well over a year after other alleged confrontations. We were in a crowded hotel lobby, and she turned and asked, why didn't I just eff off. I think I was stunned at the time and just walked out through the door. I am not really one for a confrontation when I am not instigating it.)

By Honolulu, Nic had assured me that he and Cathy were no longer an item and that he was just doing his job. When I went on to Australia, I stayed first with a friend of Nic's, Julian Dwyer, who was staying at Nic's house. I was a bit unsure about staying at Stanley Street, but Nic said it was no problem and that Cathy now had her own house. They had gone their separate ways and, even though they had appeared to be together throughout 1996, he was really just doing his job as her coach and manager and general support team and hadn't wanted to upset the boat on the eve of the Olympics. (Amazingly, they kept that weird working relationship together right up until the Sydney Olympics. It was tough, especially in Australia, because Cathy hated me, and Nic was always keeping us apart. We were both athletes, so it wasn't easy. There were big track meets in Oz. We were always needing warm-ups and always doing press conferences. We were never allowed to show up at the same time. Ever!)

I was able to move everything around and put things how I wanted them before Nic even returned to Australia! When he got back to Melbourne we went straight to the beach for a few days ... I didn't realize how big an issue it would be that we were even seen around together, so we had a secret life for a few months.

What was amazing is that every day Nic would get up at 6 a.m. and go and meet Cathy for training . . . so you can imagine the turmoil in my mind over this period of time. Nic also travelled to races with Cathy, and he did everything possible to ensure that their professional relationship continued to be successful. He even went to America for a training camp while I spent time in London and Philadelphia, but we remained in daily phone and email contact.

We did have a lot of good times and did lots of fun things away from the athletics world. One Sunday we spent the afternoon at the swimming pool in Miller Street, another of Nic's houses that we have since renovated and where we live when we are in Australia now. It was a really hot day and Nic opened a bottle of champagne he found in the fridge. The two of us and David Matthews spent the afternoon playing in the pool and drinking champagne after running for two hours in the afternoon. So it wasn't long before we were having a real laugh. It was so relaxing that we could forget all the issues which were preventing us from having a normal relationship with prying eyes all around. As the sun went down we packed up and headed back to Stanley Street. However, unbeknownst to us, there was a photographer sitting outside Miller Street looking for a story. We had gone round the corner on the way home before she even realized who we were! She had spent too much time sitting in the sun and was dozing off as we went by.

I did my training every day. Nic ran lots of runs with me and then we had fun the rest of the time.

I spent Christmas of 1996 in Melbourne. Christmas Eve was very Australian: down by the pool at Miller Street, then a pizza and a trip to the new bar down at the corner, Midnight Mass in the city, Christmas music in Stanley Street, David Matthews on a direct line to Ireland. A pretty good night.

On Christmas Day we went to see Nic's mother and then to the woods for more running. I did 1 hour 35 minutes without ever feeling too good. We had Christmas dinner with Nic's friend and accountant, Peter Jess, but by then I was tired. I slept afterwards through Christmas afternoon like an old aunt who's had one sherry too many.

A new chapter in life seemed to be beginning.

Footnote: People sometimes ask why I spell Nic without a 'k' at the end. His old newspaper byline had a 'k'. Well, the Nic I know has always been just 'Nic'. At first, when I used to write to Nic, I would write his full name, Nicholas. When I spent time with him I realized that he was not really a Nicholas, just a Nic. I know Nick was his name when he was a journalist with the *Herald Sun* . . . so I suppose I saw that as his work name and the name he had while he was with 'Voldemort'!

16

Australia in late 1996 and early 1997 was such an exciting place for me that it was easy at times to blank the Olympics from my memory. It was as if I had crawled through a hole in the fence and escaped into a happier world. I set about training in January, feeling better about myself and the future. The year got going with the usual runs in Melbourne, a 5000-metre race in Canberra and an 800 metres in Sydney. It was hot, I was in love, I had good company and was training again. All good.

There were occasional little reminders that I was still just an athlete crawling out of the wreckage, though. I went to Hobart in early February and felt really bad, completely lacking in concentration in a 3000-metre race. I ran 9:08, but I convinced myself that it was just a blip when I found myself in good form again a few days later for a 5000 metres in Melbourne.

I would have stayed in Australia forever, but Europe was calling. I had the threads of a career to pick up again. From Melbourne I went straight to Paris for the World Indoor Championships in March at the Palais Omnisports. There were no heats, just a straight final for the 3000 metres, and though I'm not a big fan of the indoor boards I decided to have a cut at it.

Gabriela Szabo, whose pale face was starting to haunt me, was making a point to everyone by not going in the 1500 metres but opting for this race with myself and Fernanda Ribeiro. As it turned out, there was an intense, soupy humidity in the arena that evening, and in some ways it felt like Atlanta all over again. I followed Ribeiro for much of the race, but with 300 to go I kicked away and left her behind. It felt great except that Szabo came too, following me as intently as a secret policeman. Smaller than me and six years younger, she was hard to shake. I was feeling good though, and so I kicked again with 120 metres left. Again she stayed there! Solemn and determined. Eventually her patience paid off. She squeezed through on the inside (my fault for leaving that gap) and won the race. I came away with a World Championship silver medal and a clear explanation for myself as to why it wasn't gold. Tactics. Tactics. Tactics.

I was content enough. Paris could have been worse. When the track season got going properly I wouldn't be letting anybody sneak inside like that, and if I kept the form and the power to kick that I had felt, well, who knew what might happen.

I hadn't lost my talents for being kicked either, though. I picked up a bronze medal for the team event at the World Cross Country Championships in Turin later in the month. Not such a happy day. It was hard to find consolations. I ran at the front of the race or close to it for the first two-thirds of the 6600 metres. When you are at the front of a big race and controlling the tempo, it's a feeling like almost nothing else. You are conscious of the people around you and behind you and it is like sitting at a poker table with an unbeatable hand. You know you are in good shape. I was starting to believe again. I had a strong hand and felt good about it. I was waiting for the moment to play it, to pull away and claim my win, when my legs betrayed me on the last of the three full laps. The legs just deserted the cause, but I think they were led on by my brain. I was so comfortable when the doubts started to trespass. Little flashbacks of bad days, concentration wandering. For a few crucial minutes my head wasn't in the race at all. As soon as I started to think too much, I was in trouble again.

I went from a position where I was one of the runners controlling and leading the race to just hanging on for ninth place individually. At one stage I was thinking how good it was to be back at the head of a field and feeling well, and then suddenly I was floating back through the group, just vanishing from the fight for medals. My friend Derartu Tulu, the former Olympic 10,000-metre champion, came through for her second title in three years.

I was happy for Derartu and for Valerie and Una, the other Irish girls, but so desolate that I hadn't run well. My collapse tore the heart out of me again. I was in Turin for the weekend, virtually on my own. Kim was there and we talked later for the first time in a long time; but in the hour after the race and before the medal presentations I wandered around with no shoulder to cry on and lots of tears to cry.

My head had gone again. No consolation could be drawn from how well I had been training if I was to come to big races and lose them in my head. There was nobody there to put an arm around my shoulder and tell me it was OK. I wanted to be happy and to appear happy for the girls in the team. A team bronze in the World Cross Country was an achievement for all of us, but the confidence I had spent months building up since Atlanta had been stripped out again. I spent a distraught hour looking for a place to hide, knowing that all those people who had been happy to see me brought down a peg or two in Atlanta would be leading the chorus asking if everyone wasn't fed up by now with Sonia and her tears.

I felt alone again and didn't know where to start rebuilding it all. Back in London the next week, I hooked up again with Alan Storey and really came to appreciate the Tuesday night track sessions with Alan's cheery group. The only pressure from Alan and the gang was to do less and to find the enjoyment again. I would go down on a Tuesday night and, though everyone worked hard at the track, there were always jokes and laughter and stories being told.

By mid April, though, it was time to migrate again. I can't stand still. I went back to Haverford, where it was cold and snowy even in April, but where I worked away happily and was joined after a short while by Nic.

Terrence was around for a while. Marcus was there. Nic was there. Surrounded by people who believed in me more than I did at the time, I began looking forward cautiously to the World Championships in Athens in August.

I ran a 1500-metre race in Oregon in May just before I came back to London. Ran well and felt good. In late May I had more tests done on myself in Limerick with Giles Warrington, the physiologist there. I was getting back to normal but was not there yet.

First communion

Graduation from Villanova

With Dick Bourke of Jury's and my sister Gillian after I was named Jury's Cork
Sports Star of the Year

The 3000-metre final at Barcelona in 1992 – I came fourth, narrowly missing a medal in my first Olympics (Inpho)

Winning my first major gold medal, in the 3000 metres at the European Championships in Helsinki, 1994 (Inpho)

An even bigger gold medal: for the 5000 metres at the World Championships at Gothenburg, 1995 (Inpho)

And two more: at Cork Airport, with my parents and my golds from the World Cross Country Championships at Marrakesh, 1998

I had never competed at 10,000 metres before, but at the 1998 European Championships in Budapest I took gold in the event as well as in the 5000 metres (Inpho)

Receiving an honorary degree from DIT, with the Taoiseach, Bertie Ahern, in 1999

Training run in
Falls Creek with
Ciara in her buggy,
January 2000

My training diary from
that month was very
neat, by my standards,
befitting the first month
of an Olympic year;
it got messier as the
months passed

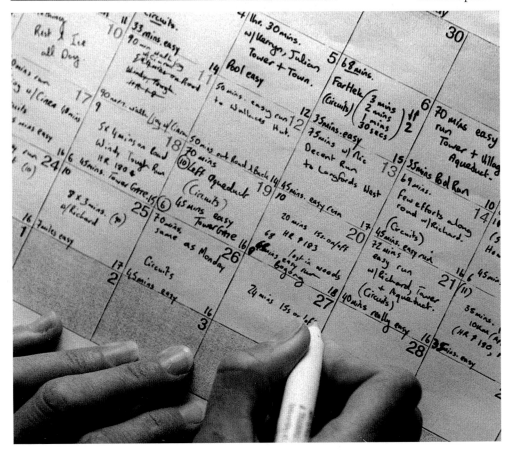

It was a great honour to carry the Irish flag at the opening ceremony of the 2000 Olympics at Sydney (Inpho)

Taking Olympic silver in the 5000 metres wasn't quite enough to erase the disappointment of Atlanta – only gold could have done that – and the margin of defeat was painfully narrow, but it was a great achievement and I knew I'd left everything on the track (Inpho)

Our tiny wedding: Nic and I were accompanied by Ciara, Sophie and two witnesses

With Nic and the girls on swings near our home in London (Mark Shearman)

With John O'Shea of GOAL, Jimmie McGee, Frank O'Mara, Ronnie Delany, Marcus O'Sullivan, Eamonn Coghlan and Ray Flynn on the 20th anniversary of the (still standing) world record in the 4 x 1-mile relay, set by Frank, Marcus, Eamonn and Ray in 1985

Training run above the clouds, Falls Creek, 2007

The summer was more turbulent than I had expected it to be, though. I ran a second place in a 1500 metres in Paris and felt decent. Less than two weeks later though, in Nuremberg, I came in second at the same distance again, but a second slower instead of faster. And by the end of June, when I ran in Sheffield, a 1500 yet again, I was some 6 seconds slower than I had been at the start of the month. I came in tenth, 13 seconds behind Kelly Holmes, who won.

So I withdrew. I turned away from the track season altogether and just started to focus on Athens, hoping that if I didn't run in track races at which I got progressively slower, well then, maybe I just wouldn't get progressively slower!

Athens sort of mugged me. I expected more of it and of myself. We arrived on Thursday night after a 3.5-hour flight and waited an age for our bags to arrive, but then we got accredited and were whisked off to the Hilton. I was staying there. Nic was in an apartment about five minutes away. The first night we went out and had, what else, a Greek salad. I got to bed early and got my head ready for the next day.

Next morning, there was a press conference hosted by Reebok. The Irish media were there in force, and I was pretty relaxed and feeling good and I sang a happy tune. I got a bus out to the stadium to have a look at the set-up for my heat the next morning; and Nic called when I was on the bus and said he was at the track and would wait to run with me.

Everything was good. We ran. Met up with Dave Matthews. Went out to the Stanley Hotel and picked up my Irish gear and race numbers (without fuss), and on the way back to the Hilton a nice policeman stopped a taxi for me. Dinner again with Nic. Just to be adventurous, we had Greek salad. I set the alarm for 5.30 a.m.

Up at 5.30 a.m. and a quick 10-minute run around the block. Athens is dark but pretty warm at that hour; the streets smell of disinfectant. Had a piece of bread and some coffee and headed with Kim and Frank on the *Track and Field News* tour bus to the track. Odd to be there at 7 a.m. with the place empty. So I just lay down behind the high jump area and relaxed for a little while.

We were at the start line at 9 a.m. and things couldn't have gone better. I felt great once we got going fast, and that was it. Job done. Through to the semi-finals. A bottle of Isostar and two bananas and back to the hotel for a 12-minute cold bath, and for lots of people the day was only just beginning. I speak to Alan on the phone; the talk is of Kelly Holmes coming off injured this morning and Svetlana Masterkova looking poor. I have a good feeling. Nic is out late. He is at the track with Cathy. Stress, but I am blanking it.

Sunday, and I am drawn in the first semi-final, which pleases me. The race is in the evening and I am tense in the afternoon but looking forward to things. I kill the warmest hours watching Eurosport and reading magazines, and finally at 6 p.m. get a bus to the stadium. There is a huge crowd in tonight because the 100-metre finals are on. The warm-up track is a little distance away but you can hear the excitement.

I try to replicate everything exactly as for the first round. In the warm-up area I even rest for a while at the high jump area. I want to set my routine for the week. When we are finally led out to the track, I feel relaxed and ready. They take a long time to start the race but finally we are away. I start a bit slowly but stay in contact. I try to stay out of trouble for as long as possible. Typically, I lose concentration during the race and lose my position for a while. Coming into the second-last bend on the final lap, I am potentially in trouble, hanging in at second-last position in the field. There is a lot of jostling. It is the sort of race you would need boxing gloves for. I feel OK though, and find a kick of acceleration to burst past five stragglers and back into contention. I look up at the screen and see I am in a qualifying position, so I relax in the home straight, which is a luxury. I'm happy.

I have finished fourth in the first semi-final of the night, a good, hard run and a tightly fought heat. It gets better. The qualifying time of 4:05.31 is the fourth fastest of the qualifiers; but the Olympic champion, Masterkova, has failed to qualify – and of course Kelly Holmes, the fastest 1500-metre runner in the world this year, pulled out of the heats, suffering from injury, on Saturday.

After the year of going backwards, after the tears and false starts and crushing sense of failure, it feels great to have battled to a major final again; I can't wait for the final on Tuesday. I get through the mixed zone (where the media meet the athletes) as quickly as possible. Nic is around to warm down with me. We talk and run quickly. Too quickly. We have to slow down and jog a warm-down!

I am so excited I can hardly sleep and have to get up for half a sleeping tablet at one stage. Next thing it is morning, the morning before a major final. Now the real racing will begin. I take the day off. Not having woken till 10.30, I don't really have a choice! I do nothing except a light jog in the park with Frank and Bob Kennedy and a couple of interviews on the roof of the hotel with RTE and the BBC, then lunch with Frank and Brendan Foster in a nice place with service so slow that lunch kills off the entire afternoon. When I get back to the hotel, Nic has already gone to the track. Cathy's final is on tonight. He is confident about it. I take another very short jog, have some fish and rice for dinner and sit down for the highlight of the night on Eurosport, the women's 400-metre final.

Funny, but knowing what Nic has been through for the previous eight months I want Cathy to win because for Nic it will be like winning a World Championship himself. He will be so relieved that it is over and that Cathy has done well. He might get a medal himself for perseverance.

At this stage I have no fight left in me as regards Cathy. I hope she can accept me as a friend and we can stop all this 'best of enemies' stuff. It will make things easier for both of us in the future. It's strange to be so nervous, watching somebody else's race. I actually got goosebumps and butterflies, the whole works. It's strange to feel a connection when you are just watching and have no control.

Cathy won and showed a lot of courage and guts running from lane one, and she got a great response. It feels like the World Championships are really on now. More exciting than ever. I go to bed but wake again after just two hours and get up to make some camomile tea with honey to help me nod off again. Nic comes in just as I am heading off with my tea; he has a gold medal in his pocket and is relaxed and happy; all the hard work has paid off for him. I hit the sack and don't wake till nine o'clock. Nic goes out to do media work with Cathy. I have a day to kill and energy to hoard for the final. I had what they call my circadian rhythms down pat now. I spent the afternoon as usual, watching Eurosport, reading, and then a light meal of fish and rice some hours before setting off to the track.

Again the stadium is buzzing. There are big sprint races on tonight and Michael Johnson is the box-office draw. It's exciting at the warm-up track, hearing the buzz of the crowd and feeling good as I try to replicate what I have been doing each time I come to the stadium.

At no time did it feel like it was going to be another bad day at the office, another episode in the Sonia soap opera. And yet it ended in eighth place and a night that just dissolved into chaos, controversy and uncertainty.

What happened? I was feeling great. I felt that I had some authority in the race as we bumped around for the first three laps. I was in a good position with about 300 metres to go. Malin Ewerlöf of Sweden had led the pack through the first 900 metres, but when the bell went for the last lap, Regina Jacobs the American and I moved up. Next thing, just as Carla Sacramento of Portugal made a move, this Swiss runner, Anita Weyermann, who was in a bad position, decided to get out of there and she pushed through a gap as if she was barging through the saloon doors in a bar in Dodge City. I was sent one way, Ewerlöf another. Regina Jacobs switched lanes. I was falling and I grabbed Regina Jacobs's vest to steady myself. I never got my rhythm back. Sacramento was gone. Jacobs caught her, led briefly but finished second. Weyermann was third.

In the tunnel afterwards I stopped to speak with Tony O'Donoghue of RTE. We had just started the interview when I was spun around by Regina Jacobs, who poked me in the chest and said, 'You cost me the gold medal, you stupid bitch.' I'm not sure what I replied, but I think it involved the words 'I', 'cow', 'falling', 'you' and 'was'.

This was as dramatic a scene as the mixed zone had seen all week. The journalists were all in a tizzy. The Swiss gathered around Anita Weyermann down the way and poked their mikes in her face. She was unrepentant, apparently. I was so surprised I ran straight by the Irish media and would have to come back later to explain it all. The Americans landed on Regina Jacobs. Her quotes were the best. 'I'm angry, very angry,' said Regina. 'I pushed her in the tunnel. If you do something as blatant as that, you don't have to act up and make a big deal about it. She should have apologized to me. Sonia was falling, she said, and she grabbed my shirt and nearly took me out of the race. She said she was falling. I think she was desperate. I had the last word. I'm on the medal stand and she's not. Nyah, nyah, nyah, nyah, nyah.'

Funny thing was that Regina was always one of those athletes that people whispered about. She fuelled it by coming up with odd excuses for pulling out of major events, either after drug testing at a US championship or at big events where tough new drug testing was sure to be in place – namely the 1995 World Championships, 2000 Sydney Olympics and the 2002 World Cross Country Championships. Then in 2003 Regina tested positive for the 'designer' steroid, THG. She got a four-year ban and, last anybody heard, she was an estate agent.

Last word, Regina? Tetrahydrogestrinone!

In Athens, after the dodgems episode, I had another shot. Two days later I went in the heats to defend the 5000-metre title I had won two years previously. The adventure ended with more pain.

I had a plan, a simple plan. I wanted to take the lead five laps out and then throw in two fast laps. But there and then on the night, when the race quickened I couldn't quicken along with it. It felt as if I was stuck to the track. I thought about stopping but then decided I couldn't do that – I had to see it through to the end. At the finish, I still had enough strength to race the last 120 metres, hoping against hope that somehow I'd get in as one of the fastest losers. But, deep down, I knew the worst without having to look at printouts of times. When you come home in seventh place in a World Championship semi-final in a time of 15 minutes 40.82 seconds, almost a full minute outside your personal best, you don't expect any miracle to save you.

And that was Athens. One last time into the mixed zone. The same old faces, leaning over the railings with the microphones in their hands, gently wondering what went wrong this time.

I told them that some people had advised me against coming to Athens and that others had taken a different view; but in the end I had been guided by my own feelings. I had done the work, I had prepared well, yet still it all fell apart for me. I accepted now that there was something wrong, but I didn't know what it was.

I stood there, looking at all these journalists, all these familiar faces, friends most of them, who had come to so many races over the years and who had leaned over railings like this and gathered around on so many good nights. And more than anything I wanted not to cry in front of them, not to have them see me walk away once again with my face streaked with tears, for that not to be the image of me back home. But they were so gentle, so delicate, so determined to collude with me in there being no upset that it couldn't last.

'I do it because I love it,' I said after an awkward little silence. 'I just love it. But it didn't work out.' And that was it. My lip quivered. I had my running shoes in my hand, the damn tears were escaping on to my cheeks and I just turned and escaped out of yet another stadium.

One more night of the same old heartache in my love affair with racing. Something would have to give.

17

Funny. Marcus used to say that people like me were like hurricanes, forces of nature that blew through people's lives and places and left a big pile of wreckage behind, but kept going. You are just so determined to get what you want, you just keep blowing on.

Athletics is a selfish life. Absolutely. For sure. And for a few years I was the best at athletics. Which meant being very selfish. Perhaps when you hit rock bottom, with everything that you lose you gain some piece of yourself back again.

When Athens was over I thought people would be fed up with my failure, tired of my tears and my dramas. After all, what was a series of personal disasters for me to everyone at home was really just some races on the television that didn't work out. Yet, as they had after Atlanta, people surprised me. Everywhere I went, people would tell me how sorry they were. In a funny way they made it all that much more sad than it actually was, just because it affected them and they shared that with me. It still chokes me up to think about it.

People spoke to me tenderly as if somebody had died, as if something was gone. It was gone, I suppose, but what was left of me started to understand a little bit more about the place I came from. And the people. What I had lost made me a bit more approachable to people. At home, on the streets or in the super-markets, people would come up to me and touch me and squeeze my arm or my hand and wish me the best.

I changed. Defeats didn't nibble away at my soul for weeks afterwards. Sure, defeats would always trouble me, but the minute, gruesome details of each loss didn't own my brain any more. To some extent the obsession was cured. I wasn't so selfish any more. Bad things happen to other people too. Worse things than losing a race or two. If you don't run well, people say, 'Sure it could be worse.' They are right, of course. Moses Kiptanui snapped a tendon in the Goodwill Games, and people would say to me that it could be worse. Look what happened to Moses, it could be worse. When you are an athlete, this idea of what might be worse than defeat shouldn't matter. There shouldn't be anything worse. Now I thought to myself, yeah, poor Moses.

I was easier to be around than before. All that had mattered in my life for years was whatever I wanted to do. Nothing else. I was still headstrong, would still take notions, but everyone around me was calmer, and so was I. Failure slows you down a little bit, makes you think that everything you are doing might not be one hundred per cent perfect and justified after all. I realize now that when you run for a living, it is very easy to get wrapped up in your own little world and think that everybody is out there looking in at you and thinking about you all the time.

After Athens I downgraded from hurricane force to maybe a tropical storm. I slowed down somewhat and took the time to look at the world I was running through. I stepped off the treadmill of aeroplane to hotel to track and back. Before that happened though, I just stepped out of the athletics world. I pulled out of the rest of the season and let my body recover. Nic and I escaped to Sicily for a holiday. The streets were all cobblestoned so you would twist your ankle if you tried to run. So we didn't run. For the first time I stopped. We swam, lay in the sun, ate whatever and drank Italian wine. There were track meets going on and results that were of vital and desperate importance to the participants in those races. We didn't even try to find out. We escaped from the world. It was perfect.

I got back to work in October. Tuesdays at the track with Alan and the group. I was training now at a different level of hardness than I had been for years. Sessions just made me tired now rather than wearing me out. For years I would feel guilty if my body didn't ache from training. For years I had needed to feel every single day that I could run faster than everyone else if a race had broken out then and there.

Alan made a big difference in my head. He took the sessions

away from me. I was no longer planning them myself or with Kim; I wasn't thinking about sessions every waking hour. I was just clocking in, doing what I was told. And it was a relief. All I had to do was follow instructions.

I'd ask Alan sometimes why I was running slower in training than I knew I could run. It was still hard to accept not going flat out. He'd just tell me that there would be a time and place to go 'eyeballs out'. Some days now I'd run home, go straight indoors and, instead of 400 sit-ups and an ice bath, I might take the hoover out for a walk around the house or cut the grass in the back garden or go for coffee and a long lunch.

I ran a 5000-metre road race that October in Edinburgh. I won it and it felt easy. Yvonne Murray followed me home. It was a small enough thing, but it gave me the encouragement to keep believing in my new way of life. There was another way of doing things which would bring results anyway. I was quite happy. More than bugs or infections or fatigue or training, that was what I needed to be. The failures and the losses were the path of life that had got me there.

I damaged my calf one day, training in late October, and we travelled to Australia in early November. I had to take things even easier for a couple of weeks. It didn't hurt to do that. I put Atlanta and Athens into a little box and threw away the key. I realized I was probably the last person on earth still thinking about those things. It was time to move on.

18

1998 was the year of putting my running life back together. I had the components; I just needed to assemble them again. Nobody gives you instructions for that sort of thing. On the first day of the year, while the world slept off its hangover, I was on a grass track in Tasmania, running a handicap race. New Year. New life. It sounded like a plan anyway.

In a handicap race they give each runner a starting mark depending on their ability. I'd run one a couple of days before and my competitive instinct started coming back to me. They gave me a mark that assumed I could run 3:58 for 1500 metres that very day. At the time I was in the sort of form that would hit 4:10 for 1500 metres if I was feeling OK. The handicap they were giving me left me no chance of winning. So . . . I harassed the judges and got what I considered to be a fair start, an extra 20 metres on. I even tried to get into the junior race. I still didn't win, but I ran half decently. Something familiar clicked into place. I was happy.

We went with the old routine after that. Got up at 6.30 a.m. to get an hour's run in before going for the plane. Back to Melbourne. A quick stop-off at Stanley Street. Unpack. Pack. And then straight to Falls Creek, five hours' drive away.

I love the ritual of going to Falls Creek, stopping at the last available supermarket for provisions that have to last a while. It's like pancakes before Lent. And then living in the Pfefferkorn Lodge with the distance-running freaks who are up there at that time of the year.

The first day up in Falls Creek I was filled with renewed spirit. And, as usual, a little too much ambition. Not long after arriving, I ran out on a bit of a session. There was a hill, a decent challenge of a hill, and though I should have known better I went along with the more macho bunch who were running up it at full pelt. However, the others had been up there in Falls Creek since Christmas, up there where the air is rare. They were used to running at 5,000 feet above sea level. I was still a landlubber. I was rewarded with pains in the head, nausea, everything. It was cold, windy and raining. I was miserable. Lovely.

We stayed in Falls Creek until the end of January, until it started to feel like we were running at sea level again. I love it up there, with the landmarks and the variety of runs and the lyrical names to the places. I run on Baby Aqueduct or Windy Corner Hill. I pelt through Langford's Gap, Howman's Gap or around Bogong Lake, or I take a long Sunday run to Pretty Valley or a bike ride to Mount Beauty. A different world. And all at least 5,000 feet above sea level.

Altitude becomes normal to you after a while, and in Falls Creek I started to push myself again. I'd do 10 miles in the morning and six in the evening. Well over 100 miles a week. My short-to-medium-term target was the World Cross Country in Marrakech in April.

Immediately after the 1500-metre race in Athens the previous summer, I was talking to Alan Storey on the mobile phone. I was down, near tears again. Alan was telling me that I needed to look forward again, to look forward to something, anything. He said specifically to look to the World Cross Country. I'm not sure if he picked that because it was far enough away for me not to become a basket case in between times, but I took that idea away from Athens, along with all the grief and confusion. Since John Treacy won back-to-back World Cross Country titles in the 1970s, the event has been special to Irish people. That was when the event started to figure in Irish imaginations. It was a perfect suggestion by Alan.

One catch. For ages I thought I was going to run the short race in Marrakech. This year is the first that there will be two separate races. So I am in Falls Creek and Alan Storey calls and mentions casually that we both know that the long race in Marrakech is the real race and that the short race is the Mickey Mouse race. That sort of piques me. I've been running around, planning for the short race, for a while now. Now he tells me this is Mickey Mouse territory. So I go off the idea of just doing the short race.

Before Marrakech, though, there was purging and suffering to be done. We'd finish running and stand up to our waists in an ice-cold rock pool. This extreme penance was supposed to be good for us. At any rate, so we told ourselves as we stood and shivered. Runners will do anything if they think it might be good for running.

Sundays in Falls Creek were days of work, the same as any other day. Sunday runs were long and hilly, excursions to way out in the middle of nowhere. Normally, runs of just over two hours to Pretty Valley. On Sundays I'd run by myself, just going for miles, nobody in sight but cows. Funny, the things that make you home-sick. The cows would remind me of home and Cobh and wet days dodging cowpats in the fields; but then again, meeting the cows when I was out on my own in the middle of nowhere was spooky and not sentimental. They half scared the life out of me. I half scared them to death too. Every once in a while a couple of them would fail to get out of the way and they'd run along, panicked and dozy, crapping all over the place, me behind them, splashing about in it.

I had exactly four weeks at Falls Creek and then I came back to the real world. I was eager to test the value of Falls Creek. I road-tested the legs at sea level. A good run out around Melbourne. So disappointing. I thought I would be scorching the earth, but I felt nothing special in the legs at all. My faith in hard work was slightly shaken.

I tried a weekend cross-country race in Canberra. The Aussie capital is a cool, strange city, full of government buildings and modern architecture. Everyone in the city goes home for the weekend, leaving this eerie ghost town behind them. The race snaked through the flat, perfect gardens of Parliament House. Sunny and surreal and quiet.

The race was three laps of two kilometres. I decided to run the first lap with everyone else, see how they were going and how I was going. I felt good, so I stretched the legs for the second lap. Then I went away on the third lap. Falls Creek kicked in at last. I won by about 30 seconds and was happy with it all. A time of 20 minutes 21 seconds, and then a 70-minute warm-down. It all seemed good, but you never really know with cross-country.

Next, I went to Auckland. It's a strange life when you stop to think about it. I got up early in Melbourne for a 50-minute run at 6.30 a.m. Flew to New Zealand and immediately set into sit-ups, push-ups and a 50-minute run around the fields. That's how I form impressions of places: arriving and running around.

Auckland was wet and windy. The streets and the houses piled together in muted colours. Auckland is like a lot of Irish towns and I loved the feel of the place. I won a 3000-metre track race by 30 seconds. Put in a last lap of 64 seconds. I liked the feel of Auckland even better then.

The race in Auckland was on a Saturday. On Thursday it was back to Oz for a 5000 metres in Melbourne, a race with Grand Prix points attached. Another 30 seconds' margin, but this time, for the first time in the year, actually in a half-decent race. For the first time in a long time I was beginning to believe that I had turned a corner.

I was feeling good. Marcus was down there gathering sub-4-minute miles to bring his tally closer to 100. I was running with him most days, like a tour guide exploring a Melbourne that was now becoming my new hometown. After Melbourne I was raring for more competition and I knew there was a race on Saturday in Sydney. It hadn't been decided whether I should run it or not, but I had the feeling that if I was winning all these races by 30 seconds, I'd better find something a bit more competitive, and soon. I was feeling good; but after the previous two years everyone was worried for me taking on three races in a week. They'd seen me look like one of those cartoon characters before, the ones who keep on running after they have gone out over the edge of the cliff, but then drop like a stone. Alan was telling me that I didn't need to run, but if I was sure it wouldn't hurt me, then to perhaps do it. Marcus was more doubtful. He thought I was getting too greedy too quickly. He remembered me racing almost to a standstill in the seasons before Atlanta. I argued for just one more race before Europe. I had a motive up my sleeve.

Sydney was a 1500-metre race. My old friend from Athens, Regina Jacobs, would be in the field. Jacobs had run an 800 in Melbourne and ran it well. She and I hadn't spoken since we'd almost come to blows in the stadium in Greece the previous summer. There was stuff to settle. I convinced everyone, including myself, that I could run the race and that would be the end of it. I was cool about it. I went off to see U2 play the night before. On the afternoon of the race I blew Jacobs away on the last bend. It was 28 February. Rolling. Rolling. Rolling. This was going to be a good year.

Twelve days later, I travelled back to London. I trained on a Thursday morning at the track in Melbourne. Got in early on Friday morning and stayed awake all day. When I got tired that evening, I went out for a run, 45 minutes in Bushy Park. It woke me up. I slept that night and got back into the rhythm and, while absorbing the jet lag, I got used to the way things were back at base now.

After Atlanta, my little world around Teddington had needed to be rebuilt. When my relationship with Kim changed, it had a larger effect than just a personal one. What we'd had just wasn't working, but I felt that, as a great agent and influence, he still had the power to do things for me. I needed him in lots of little ways, but it had been the intensity, the overwhelming obsession with running, that wasn't helping either of us.

I'd asked could he, well, kinda advise me, kinda coach me. He'd said no. It was all or nothing. A very Kim response. So it was nothing. It was a very awkward time. Later, when Nic had come on the scene, I didn't want him to get into that ABC position. Agent. Boyfriend. Coach.

1997 had been an up-and-down sort of year. I was happy in general, and that allowed me to run well sometimes; but the Athens World Championships had been a disaster and had made me realize that coming back to where I had been wouldn't be easy. You can't just go with the flow and assume that everything will work out.

Things changed, with me being more friendly with Kim just before Christmas. We made the trip to Australia once again through Honolulu, stopping off for the Nike road race. All through 1997 I hadn't wanted to talk to Kim or be with him, but he was around the place all the time, and mostly I couldn't avoid him. I used to feel that if he was asking me about training he was being judgemental. It was the most I could do to answer him vaguely. In Honolulu he cornered me and told me to decide what I wanted. 'Do you want to have nothing to do with me, or do things properly and communicate? It doesn't work otherwise.'

He was right. By then a little bit of the anger and hurt had gone out of the Olympic experience for me. When we spoke in Honolulu I realized that he was still interested and concerned about me as an athlete and a client, and I had been suffering because I just couldn't accept the help. In relation to the Olympics, what had happened between us was perhaps not as big a deal as people thought. Some said it was all Kim's fault, and tabloids reported that there had been a big fight between us and all that. Nothing like that had happened; and if it had, it wouldn't have had anything to do with running. I was in a frame of mind back then where it was easy for me to block out anything emotionally.

Kim agreed with that way of operating, and that's the way we operated. It was simple to do that. If there were little tensions, they were professional more than personal. In my training in America the whole thing was building up with disagreements, when I was starting to feel bad coming up to the races. I wasn't happy with running. When Kim and I had started, my career was all fresh and everything was new. That got old after a while though, and problems with running and not feeling good at training came home. In Honolulu Kim made a sensible suggestion about what was best for my career. I came back from Australia, looking forward to spending more time working with him again and talking to him a bit more after the World Cross Country.

I hadn't seen much of Kim from the end of 1997 onwards but,

as it happened, he was travelling to Morocco with Bob Kennedy and myself. Bob, Kim and I had a 50-minute run together, the day before we travelled. It broke the ice and felt like old times in some ways, getting ready for a big race and plotting and planning and talking. As far as I was concerned, I felt like part of the team we had had before. Things were the way they used to be, but now I had my distance and my own space. Things were separate but they were good. Kim was always excellent with advice, and it felt natural listening to him and his opinions on the races and the people competing. He was always so certain about things that it was easy to believe him when he spoke about athletics.

The next day we travelled to Marrakech via Gibraltar and Casablanca. We arrived in Morocco in the middle of the night and I checked into the wrong hotel, some dive down a back alley; it was dirty and scary. Kim, who specialized in getting the best accommodation for his athletes, was feeling his blood pressure rise, so I checked out again and went with Kim and Bob to the hotel they had booked well in advance. La Mamounia! A gorgeous, stately old hotel which was Winston Churchill's favourite and the place where he came to write his memoirs. It had a good track record. Kim was vindicated. It was the ideal spot to launch a campaign from!

They were happy days, when I felt good again and willing to be distracted by running. It was as if all the tension between us was gone. I was more relaxed, less worried about anything than I had been in a long time, and happy to be in their company again.

When we got up the next morning, we talked through the problems – food, heat – and then ran for 40 minutes. Always in a new place we just come out and ask which direction the course is in and then head that way. So that Friday morning Kim brought me to an IAAF press conference and then we surveyed the course.

That sounds like a small thing, a press conference, but after two years of being in the wilderness and on my own most of the time, just to spend some time sitting in front of a room full of people who were at least pretending, for professional purposes, to be interested in me and my career was a tonic. Sometimes you need to feel like a star. Kim had the power and influence to slot people in and out of press conferences pretty much as he wished. He knew that it would be good for me and my confidence to be there, and I came away with a little bit of what it used to feel like to be a star.

Afterwards we had a jog around the course, which was being watered at the time. The sun was shining and the terrain was all olive groves. People were everywhere doing odd jobs. There were mad, frantic scenes unfolding everywhere you looked. My mind at that stage was still only on one event, the 8-kilometre race the following day.

It pays to prepare, especially in a race with as many variables as a cross-country has. What I saw and absorbed on Friday probably helped me cope with the tale of the unexpected which we had the next day. To begin the race, they put us into these large wooden stalls or pens, like horses or cattle. There was general confusion – and then they started the race without saying anything or warning anyone! There was no chance to think about it or to edge up to a tape and jockey for position. No chance even to think, really. Everyone just burst out of these odd wooden stalls and out across the dust and grass. We were running before we knew it.

The Kenyans went flying off at top speed. There was half a mile to this wooden ramp that we had to go over, and the pace didn't calm till then. You could get stuck behind a hundred people. I was beginning to get worried. And then for some reason it calmed, the Kenyans dropped down through the gears and they cantered as if they were in training. You could feel the relief spreading through the pack. When a race slows like that, it changes the odds, but everything is still a gamble. Either the Kenyans were nervous or they had hoped to get such a jump on the field that they would burn the rest of us off early. When it didn't happen that way, it meant that the real race had just been postponed till later. Soon, everyone was running along like in a training session. And I just felt good and kept nagging myself to do my job. Keeping up. Keeping up. Waiting for the moment.

As we all knew it would, the pace quickened on the last lap.

Paula Radcliffe, the Kenyans, a few Ethiopians all looked around, waiting for someone to make a jump. I did the job I had set out to do: just kept on keeping up, keeping up. The last half of the last lap got hard. People started kicking on. Every contender had to make her play now. I kept going, just stayed with it, and I noticed suddenly that everyone who was making it hard for me was tired and – miracle of miracles! – I wasn't tired. I just had to make up my mind. Just try and get to the finish first. Just find some of the old pace and go. It worked. When I put the foot down I was the only one who had any fuel left. I never imagined that winning it would be so easy.

Nor did I imagine that winning it would be so hard. Kim was standing just over the line when I crossed it. Typical Kim, he had a phone in his hand and he was talking to Alan Storey. The phone got handed to me. So I spoke to Alan. I never mentioned the next day's race. I was still entered in both races, but retaining the entry to the second race had been an emotional fallback, something that would give me the chance to get back up on the horse the next day if it had all unravelled in the long race. Now in any case I had a firm idea in my head.

I went away for a warm-down and the emotion welled in me. Suddenly I just cracked. The time of loneliness, the occasions of being in places like this and feeling so alone and isolated and abandoned were over. Maybe this sounds shallow, but when your job defines you as much as being a runner does, you need some self-esteem. The press swarming about, officials leading me here and there, people pumping my hand, tricolours flying – suddenly I appreciated all the fuss. These were things I had once taken for granted. Sometimes you don't know what you've got till it's gone.

In the chaos, my bag which had my mobile phone in it went missing. It should have been back at the starting area where I'd left it, but when I got back there it was gone. I spent half the day looking for it and making inquiries about it. I got a little time to sit and chat with Bob Kennedy and I fell to thinking more seriously about running the next day, half thinking that I wouldn't bother, half knowing that nothing would stop me.

I knew that some people were against me running it, but here I was. I had won. I had my plan. I had no phone. Why make a big deal out of it? So I just didn't call anyone. I thought to myself that there were scheduled to be four cross-country champions coming out of Marrakech. To make sure that there were only three people going home with winners' medals would be something different, something memorable.

So it was only when I was walking to the start for the short race the next morning that I rang Alan Storey to tell him. I was more nervous about telling Alan than I was about running the race. I knew that this was a moment in our athlete–coach relationship that he would have to swallow. I was telling him rather than asking him. He paused. I told him it was only a bonus. I said if it was tennis, I'd have won the singles, and sure, this is just the doubles. I promised him I wouldn't be upset if I lost.

I didn't lose. I rang him afterwards, and Alan just said that he was glad there was no mixed doubles.

I'd got away with it.

19

Marrakech changed a lot of things for me. Or, more correctly, I suppose I was very much changed by the time Marrakech happened. I learned to enjoy victories just as much as I had tortured myself in defeats. I look back on my diary from 1995 when I won the World Championships in Gothenburg, and I am not sure what I was thinking of, going on without skipping a beat. I reacted to Gothenburg as something which I had always expected to happen, and I played it down both in my own head and to the world outside. Gothenburg had been just a relief more than anything. I was expected to win the World Championships. I won the World Championships. I can tell in the pictures from the events how happy I was at the time. In Gothenburg my face sort of says, 'Look, I knew I could do it anyway.' Marrakech was different. Real happiness. I went with the flow. I knew enough by then to know that there are only so many chances that you get in a career. And no more.

And I knew what my new mantra was in every race. I would have to think about every race, every time. Ask myself that question, 'Do I want this? And can I concentrate enough to take it?'

In Marrakech I remember the Moroccan officials whisking me off to shake hands with the late Primo Nebiolo, who was head of the IAAF at the time. 'Thees is heestoric moment,' said Primo, and the pair of us stood there, shaking hands and grinning awkwardly. It was something the old Sonia would never have got involved in, but now I felt like I was back in the centre of things again.

And not long afterwards I found myself in America. Nike flew me to their headquarters in Beaverton, Oregon, and when I got there they had a big banner up across the campus: 'Welcome Sonia O'Sullivan – World Cross Country Champion'. It struck me then, and not for the first time, that I was enjoying this little burst of glory more than I had enjoyed anything in the good years before Atlanta.

There were little problems, of course. When I won in Marrakech, Kim was there at the finish. He was available and quotable, so naturally all the journalists gathered around and spoke to Kim. He spoke of the double triumph as if it was largely his doing: Sonia's resurrection and my part in it! I don't think he meant anything by it. I didn't care anyway. I was too happy to care.

But Alan went berserk. Journalists drew the conclusion that I was running well because Kim and I were back on good terms again. Nic was going a little mad too. Here I was, back from the dead careerwise, and, just by being in the right place at the right time, Kim was mopping up all the credit. Kim didn't worry. I didn't worry either. If Nic wanted to be there, he could have been there; but he was in Australia, looking after Cathy Freeman. He had made his choice. At the time I was constantly advising him to sever his connections with Cathy as things were so stressful. I had no sympathy with his position; and if Alan had wanted to be there he could have been, but for some reason he wasn't. OK, going to Marrakech is a big deal, and I didn't expect him to be there, and nor did I need him to be there; but at the same time it was really nice to have somebody who was there, somebody to talk to and somebody to share it with. I had been to enough places all alone on bad days.

After Marrakech, the phone started to ring again. You have two bad years and commercially you go cold as a corpse. Winning the World Cross Country titles brought me back to the land of the living. For a while everyone wanted a piece of me. It was great. I went out and did everything, even interviews. Even the welcome home to Ireland, I did it my way, no more open-top buses or awkward stages; this time, with some help from my friends at Irish Guide Dogs for the Blind, I decided to run from Cork to Cobh and wave to people on the side of the road. My arms were close to falling off by the time we reached Cobh. This was my stage and I was doing what I do best, simply running!

Appearances in stores. Coaching clinics. Then I got tired of it again. Maybe not so much that I got tired of it, but I realized that I was starting to make all these things fit into the time that I had and not into the time that people thought I had. There was training to be done and a track season to face.

I went to America for a while. Did the Nike thing. Skipped down to San Francisco for a few days, took in that cool grey city and hung around, running the hills of Stanford. Did Philly. By mid April I was back in London and back to work properly, though looking forward to the track season and the European Championships in August.

I sat down with Alan to look at the track season and decide which races to do. I made all my bad decisions for the year in one swoop. I looked too far ahead too soon. You are given a list and you decide. I didn't look at it from a technical point of view, and it was Alan's first season with me. I agreed to do all these races. Later it was difficult to unagree them.

The Golden League system which athletics was constantly tampering with at that time meant that it made most sense to enter a lot of 1500-metre races. So we picked a series of them, but we continued our training regime which was geared towards the longer distances. We sat and looked at the schedule of track meets, and I was filled with excitement because I was back and I wanted to be in all those places, going in big races again. Mistake! Pretty soon I wanted to go and redraw the entire schedule and pick the races I went in all over again.

My training tried to accommodate the schedule in some way, but I started on a Thursday night in early June with a 5000 metres in St Denis, where I came third. It was the same old rollercoaster. As soon as I had run the 5000 in St Denis I knew it was going to be difficult. I'd done OK (15:03) and finished behind Ouaziz and Wami, but it was the wrong race for me. I ran a 1500 the following Tuesday in Bratislava and ran well (one second over 4 minutes, and I felt strong and good) without winning the thing and convinced myself that I was in good enough shape but not quite ready for the 5000 metres yet. The time was my best over the distance in two years. The sort of encouragement I always cling to. Run well and everything is fine; just keep going. Run badly and there is something wrong. Run well and you are cured.

I was up and down and sort of self-conscious. Winning in Marrakech was one thing but the track was where I used to be invincible. I knew people were looking at me for signs. Would I be back as strong as in the years before Atlanta, or was I on the verge of cracking? I knew a lot of people would lose faith in me very quickly. There she goes again! What next?

I was sort of naive. I was going well, but I knew in my heart that I should have been better. I hadn't trained as well as I should have and a few niggling injuries had hobbled me. But you go out on to the circuit and that is it, the momentum pulls you along. Here. There. Everywhere.

Soon I was going to tracks and places that were all too familiar, and when I got there I would realize that I hadn't missed them quite like I'd thought I would; I'd been in too many of these places too many times before. I kept asking the question: 'Am I interested? Do I want this?' A lot of the time the answer was, 'No, not really.'

I went to Oslo and got thrown around the place in a donkey derby of a race. I came fourth, which seemed really disappointing after all the good nights in Oslo. I ran a 4:03 and got lost around the streets of Oslo doing my warm-down. It could have been worse, as I found out a few days later.

On to Rome. Another 1500-metre race. Came in ninth and felt bad. But I always found fuel to fan the flames of delusion. Two nights later, I ran a 3000 metres in Nice and felt pretty good, even if I had no zip at the end of it.

In July I was home for the BLE National Championships. I had entered the 800, the 1500 and the 5000 metres at the championships, but by the time I arrived in Dublin I had decided to do just the 5000.

Dad wanted to come up and collect me at the airport, but I told him to get sense; I'd get a taxi. I hit Dublin airport and holiday-makers were swarming all over the place like ants. The queue for taxis stretched to infinity and beyond. But people are so nice: I came out and everyone ushered me into a car straight away as if I was on emergency call at a hospital. The driver asked for an autograph instead of a fare. A couple of minutes later, we were at Morton Stadium, down in Santry. People are so nice – and then again some people are so BLE.

The BLE official radiated the usual attitude towards me.

'Nine pounds please.'

'Huh?'

'You're entered for three events – three each please.'

'But I'm only running one event!'

'Still nine pounds.'

'Hmmm.'

Great to feel special!

I won the 5000 at home in Santry, but by the time I got to Budapest in August the only two races which I had won out of the ten I had entered all summer were at home in Ireland. Elsewhere I was a disaster.

But I kept telling myself that I had a plan. That strong run in Nice set me up again. On and on. Just as typical of the summer, I suppose, was my defeat to Paula Radcliffe in a low-key 3000-metre race at Sheffield. I dropped off a modest pace at a fairly early stage and Paula beat me by the length of the finishing straight in the end. I got distracted somewhere along the way. Same old problem.

I went to Zurich, the last big race before the Europeans. I finished seventh in the 1500 metres but wasn't disappointed. I put in a 4.02 for the 1500, which was round about my average for the year and I started to conclude, rightly or wrongly, that my policy of training for the longer races in Budapest but running shorter races all summer had some sense to it. At the track on Tuesdays with Alan's group and following his instructions between times, I had laid down the basis for a challenge in the longer races. All the 1500-metre outings on the circuit I treated as speed training and dismissed in my head where I finished in the race.

In Zurich, for instance, I did an hour on the track when the meet finished. I just treated the whole thing in my head as a training day. I did 35 minutes in the morning and an hour afterwards and felt good all the time.

Budapest was just a week away. I had been vague all summer about my intentions there, but when I originally looked at the timetable the 10,000 metres had taken my fancy and I had never really got past the idea of having a crack at the longer distance and then having the 5000 metres in reserve later in the week.

When I spoke to people about the 10,000 metres, which I had never run before, a lot of people tended to point out gently that if I couldn't keep my concentration for the seven and a half laps of a 3000-metre race in Sheffield against Paula Radcliffe, how did I hope to stay alert for the 25 circuits of a championship 10,000-metre race? I would begin to explain. And then forget what I was going to say!

Anyway, I wasn't for changing. The 10,000 metres in Budapest had been taking up most of the space in my imagination for a while. I like new things. Ribeiro, the Olympic champion, was going to be racing. I liked the challenge. And I took the attitude that I had nothing to lose. It was half an hour out of my life. No heats to run or anything.

I went out to Budapest on 17 August, a Monday. I trained twice on the day before I went: a session in the morning, an easy run in the evening, and that wrapped it up. Nothing more I could do.

In Budapest I collected my gear from the team hotel and vanished back to the Hotel Kempinski, where I became unavailable to everyone. I had decided for a change to keep a low profile with the media guys. To do the talking on the track, as they say.

I think I knew that it would go well. I was tuned in. I liked Budapest and running along the river, back and forth across the beautiful bridges. The 10,000 was early in the week. I had decided on my only tactic for the race: to keep up for as long as possible. I wasn't going to do anything different from what the others were doing unless they started walking. I'd never run it before, but maybe that wasn't a bad thing.

On the night in the Nepstadion I was so calm. Like a lot of

championship races, the first half was slow. After just four laps, the field had split into two groups. Myself, Ribeiro, Lidia Simon of Romania, Paula Radcliffe and Olivera Jevtic of Yugoslavia had opened up a good gap of 25 metres on the rest. The Spanish girl, Julia Vaquero, worked really hard and caught up with us some time later, but basically the winner was always going to come from that group which broke away early.

Maybe my reputation as a beaten docket was working for me at this stage. We took a leisurely 16 minutes 8.35 seconds to reach the halfway mark. As the person in the field who potentially had the fastest kick at the end of the race, they should have been trying to burn me off or lose me. I think they were gambling on me burning myself off again. My mind wandered a little but mainly just to tell myself that this wasn't bad at all. I knew that the pace would pick up for the second 5000 metres, and it did. Paula Radcliffe, knowing that she hadn't really got a kick of speed to use at the end, began to run a little more aggressively.

When we got to about 7000 metres, Vaquero made a break which nearly left me behind. I had been making a point of hanging in third or fourth spot as we went along. The night was incredibly hot but I felt very comfortable and had settled into a rhythm. When Vaquero went, I found myself slipping a couple of places and had to snap out of it. I did. I picked it up. Stayed in touch and the pace settled again.

I was comfortable and I knew I looked comfortable. On bad nights I tighten up, my face gets this horrible sheen of sweat and my features go tight. In the good times I could defeat myself and grind out a win even when I was feeling bad, but nowadays I have to feel good. I do. I know that Radcliffe and Ribeiro will have noticed too. They'll try to bump me off before the finish.

On laps twenty and twenty-one they both make their moves. Paula first. Off she goes, her head bobbing in that unusual style as she makes a little surge. She gets tracked down, and then Ribeiro goes, testing our strength. She is a tough customer, Ribeiro, and even though I lead the chase to catch her she keeps trying to shift up and down the gears for a while to see if I have the focus to stay with her. I have my simple plan, though: just keep up. Just keep up.

Everything worked. We got to the bell with me in third place and feeling strong behind Ribeiro and Radcliffe. I knew then it was over. So did the girls. I waited till we were 180 metres from home and then asked my legs to do their thing. I took the lead for the first time, going past Ribeiro like I was being carried on the wind. I'd made breaks like this hundreds of times before in races, but not one of them felt better than this. Ribeiro came in second, three seconds behind. Lidia Simon was third, Paula fifth.

I enjoyed this one so much. Jumping about the place like a kid. Punching the air! Maybe the sweetest, happiest moment of my career till then.

I ran home from the stadium that night and turned my thoughts greedily to the 5000. The world had turned. Everyone thought I should run the 5000 metres now. As late as this afternoon before the 10,000, people were counselling me not to even think about running both races. I stayed away from the track for the rest of the week, watched Dieter Baumann on the box. He went in the men's 5000 after the 10,000. Didn't go so well. Hmmm. Maybe people were right the first time.

But the field for the 5000 wasn't all that daunting. The more I looked at it, the more I felt there was a medal there for the taking. The biggest threat was the little Romanian who seemed to crop up everywhere, Gabriela Szabo. I fancied having a go at Szabo. And I had a plan!

It was a blustery Sunday afternoon for the 5000 final. I tucked in on Szabo's shoulder and played it just like the 10,000. Keep up, Sonia, just keep up. After a first lap which was so slow that we could have walked it, Szabo led us through a quick second lap which split the field. Szabo, myself, Marta Dominguez and Anne-mari Sandell settled in for a long war of attrition at the front. I hung in behind Szabo. She kept urging me to go past her and share some of the running up front. I kept ignoring her. I could tell it was getting into her head.

Afterwards she would moan about this not being fair play. That

I had let her do all the hard work. She was right in a way, but she had taken on the responsibility of front running. When you do that, you have to be prepared for anything. You can't assume that the responsibility will be shared until such time as you decide to make a break. Anyway, Szabo felt bad and didn't talk to me for quite a long time after that race. She had her chance. My mind was elsewhere when Szabo made a break with 500 metres to go. Suddenly I had dropped to fourth place. Not good. She didn't get away far enough or quick enough though, and within about 30 metres I had tracked her down and we had settled into our old pattern of her running and me stalking. We stayed that way till the last bend. I kicked, gave a quick glance over my shoulder to register her face, and left Szabo behind as I went for broke.

It took a little while for this one to register. At first I was just relieved. The 5000 was more familiar territory than the 10,000 and I knew how good Szabo was. To have hung on her shoulder for most of the race and then to have lost would have been a humiliation. This was a reprieve.

The tears came as the tricolour was run up the flagpole in the Nepstadion and for the second time in four days the strains of 'Amhrán na bhFiann' filled the place. After two years of pain it was all purged there and then. Twice in a week I had beaten good fields and great champions. There had been times when I had wondered whether I would ever stand on a track with athletes of that calibre again. To stand on the podium at a major championship and to have great athletes on either side of me was a dream I hadn't dared have for a long, long time.

Two other things I remember about Budapest. I think that is where texting started for me. Never knew it existed. Then somebody got on to me with some rumour about somebody being on drugs. Two signs of the times rolled into one. When I left Budapest my calves were tight from running so many laps of the track.

As usual, it was all business after a major championship. I took a quick trip back to London to get Gerard to sort out my calves, do some washing and get back to running my old route, just to do one of my own runs. I did a quick trip to Dublin on the night the team came home. I met them on the runway. Just got off my plane across the tarmac and on to their plane. Then got off their plane straight away out through the front door. Ta da! Here we are.

That night of the 5000 made Szabo an enemy for me. She argued that she had stepped out once or twice for me to go in front. A little while later, in the Grand Prix in Berlin, herself and a few of the girls got me in a 5000-metre race and pointedly gave me a good beating. I ran 14:51 on the night. I had hoped to do about 14:31. Szabo, Ouaziz and Wami ran brilliantly, relegating me to the depths. I had expected so much out of that night. The leaders were so far ahead I knew I hadn't a chance. It was one of those things. I was upset at the time, but their little display of strength was a minor setback. Berlin, though, was the start of the silly epilogue to that season. I had just got to the point where I was running to beat these other girls. I was determined that they wouldn't beat me, but they left me for dead.

I stayed on in Berlin on Wednesday and Thursday. It was horrible, hanging around and mulling over it when you've run really badly and don't want to be there. Looking back, I know what I should have done. Rationally, I should have gone home. I had two European medals. Two World Cross Country medals. It was enough for any year. Instead, I went to Moscow for the Grand Prix final. I ran useless altogether. Just crap.

The following day Nic wanted me to run to Red Square with him. I didn't want to go, but out of habit I was putting on my running clothes. Eventually we went out and it took maybe 55 minutes. I was really dragging on the way there, complaining about everything. Moaning. On the way back, even though I liked Red Square, I realized that I had just about had it. No more running. Then I had this idea about the World Cup on the way back. What if I don't feel like the World Cup in four years' time? That will be the last one I can enter. So I decided there and then to go to the World Cup. And in the last five minutes of the run I felt better already.

★

167

I came back to London and yet again spoke softly to Alan Storey about hard things. I convinced him, and two days after the Red Square episode (a Sunday) I was on a plane to Johannesburg, where I ran a 5000 metres in the slower than slow time of 16 minutes 24 seconds the following Saturday. I remember arriving in the hotel in Johannesburg, lying in the sun for an hour, and then not seeing the sun again all the time I was there. That summed it all up, really.

In Moscow I had also heard from Brendan Foster about the Great North Run in Gateshead. Brendan sent an invite, seeing that Liz McColgan wasn't running and the field needed some 'sparkle'. So, going to the World Cup, I decided on the climax to my season. I ran hard for an hour and a half the day after the 5000 metres in South Africa. Harder than the race was. I was training now for something new and different: the Great North Run.

In between I went to the All-Ireland football final in Dublin. Did a lap of Croke Park for GOAL. Nic and myself stayed the weekend with John Treacy, a good, happy time. I remember we went for a run out from John's house and got hopelessly lost. I was convinced we had touched on the edge of Wicklow before we asked a local to point us in the direction back to Dublin. I wasn't too worried and didn't care too much either, so long as we made it back for the start of the game!

The European part of my year finished happily. I loved the Great North Run. I just ran along for the first part of the race; then, when I knew I was comfortable and within my range of racing distances, I finished strongly into the cold north-east wind and rain along the South Shields sea-front, crossing the line in 71:50. The time didn't mean much to me as I was still too focused on track times. I was just happy to win the race and complete a new challenge.

Again I took a little time out and enjoyed myself, I took things in, went to Manchester to do *A Question of Sport*. Michael Owen was on it. It made me feel old.

And then we headed for Australia. Another chapter done and dusted, this one filed from deep in the land of the second chances.

20

Eventually we headed down to Australia. Returning there at the end of each year gives you a chance to divide the years and the seasons up and to measure one against another. After 1996 and 1997, this had been a really good year. By the time we were making our way southwards again on 29 October it had been decided that the following year would be a quiet one. And a different one.

Naturally, back in Australia there was the usual curiosity about what I was going to do for the 1999 season. The usual questions. I ran in a fun run on Australia Day, 26 January, and I won. I remember that took the pressure off for a few weeks.

Quickly enough, though, the news was out: I was pregnant. If I thought that life would never be the same again after my first Olympic final in Barcelona or after the disasters of Atlanta, here was an event coming down the track which was sure to lurch my existence in a new direction.

Things changed almost immediately but not drastically. People (hello, Mother!) insisting I take things easy. Me listening to other voices. When we came back from Australia in the spring I took a week off; but Brenda, my friend I'd been doing gym sessions with in Australia, had also arrived back in London so we went every day to the Lensbury Club in Teddington. We did plenty of gym work and as much time as we could on the stationary bicycles.

Afterwards I walked home with the stopwatch on. That provided a shock. It was the first time I'd walked that journey instead of running it and I decided that it was easier to be running. I spoke to my old friend Alison Wyeth, whom I used to train with in Isleworth and Brunel College when she lived in London. Alison had since become a mother and we chatted about the business of training during pregnancy. She told me about the things she did, how she felt when running. She told me about heart rates, wearing a monitor and keeping it below 160 beats all the time.

Then I sent a fax to Liz McColgan, who told me that she stopped running about six weeks before the birth of her daughter because she got to a point where she felt she'd done enough and was just going to sit back and enjoy the rest. Liz got back into training 11 days after having the baby, and she ran in the World Cross Country less than four months later. She finished second. Eleven days! It sounded impressive. She even ran a road race within a month of the birth. It showed me what was possible. People kept stressing that everyone is different, though; you can't compare one person's experience to the others'. So I just concentrated on keeping fit and enjoying it.

I went to Wimbledon on the day Ciara was due. I saw a little bit of Tim Henman playing before the rain came. Centre Court, front row seats – and it had to rain. Play stopped. Wandering around the place, I ran into John Inverdale of the BBC. As usual, they were trying to fill in time while it was raining, so he had me do a little chat with him. In the middle of the interview he said: 'Sonia, I believe you're seven months pregnant.'

'Seven months? No, I'm due today.'

And so the whole of Wimbledon knew and braced itself. I thought I might work the interview to my favour, though. Having been rained off the first day, I asked Inverdale if he could get a ticket for the following day. Somehow he scrounged one up. Next day, of course, it rained all day long. No tennis. Not a ball played. Optimistic as ever, though, I went down on my own in the train. Wasted a day in the rain at Wimbledon. Couldn't even get up the nerve to find Inverdale and look for another ticket.

I tried to keep going all the way to the end. Over in the gym they'd be surprised every day when I would walk in. 'Have you not had that baby yet?'

My diary for July of 1999 is the usual pages comprising small squares, all filled in with training reports.

Thursday 8 July: Bike 90 mins. Swim 20 laps. Into hospital tonight.
Friday 9 July: Hospital all day and night.
Saturday 10 July: Ciara Born @ 2:20 a.m. Easy walk 2 miles.
Sunday 11 July: walk to Richmond Park w/Nic's mother Anne 2–3 miles.

Ciara had presented herself not long after two o'clock in the morning. A little while later, Nic phoned my parents in Cobh to tell them the news. Somehow or other the news was on RTE at nine o'clock that morning. I haven't a clue how that happened. A few of the midwives in the hospital were Irish, but I can't imagine them putting in phone calls to RTE at that hour of the morning. Somebody told somebody, though.

It made for a small complication, too. I got up that morning and needed a bit of fresh air. Ciara was fast asleep and the nurses said, 'You can go outside if you like.' Never having been in hospital before, I misunderstood them slightly. So I decided to walk down to the newsagent's. Nic's mother was downstairs in the hospital and Nic had gone to the airport so, rather than sit in the room waiting for Ciara to wake up, we went for a walk to Richmond Park. I felt a little sore, but I had expected to feel a lot worse.

I didn't know at the time that the news had been on RTE. So while I was out, the switchboard lit up with Sunday papers and other people calling to find out more. With the switchboard starting to jam, the head sister came outside, looking for me, and discovered I was missing. She went frantic. Missing patient, everyone looking for me, and me walking around Richmond Park in the sunshine with Nic's mother. When I got back, I heard the head sister on the phone hassling security. I told her that I'd never done anything like that before and didn't know the rules. I wasn't popular!

Ten days late and 13 hours of labour, but Ciara was well worth the wait. At 8lb 2oz she was a big baby, but what struck everyone was how long she was. An athlete! A runner! The first set of clothes we put on her fitted her perfectly. People were wondering where Nic and I had been hiding her.

She had a stressful arrival, which left her breathing a little rapidly. The doctors were worried that she might have an infection, so they kept her in for observation after they discharged me. The hardest thing about that first week was having to leave Ciara in the hospital every evening. Every day, though, she got perkier, and on Saturday 17 July, a week later, my diary reads: Walk to track, Home from Hospital with Ciara (5 miles).

A baby brings you into the community of your friends more than anything else. All my Kenyan friends from the track were keen to see Ciara. Nic and I thought her name sounded like that of a Brazilian footballer ('Pele to Ciara – Goal!') but Moses Kiptanui called around and he thought she should be named Jemutai, which means one who arrives in the early hours of the morning.

I read a book somewhere along the way about the great Ingrid Kristiansen. Ingrid trained until the very day she gave birth, and she was running again 10 days later. Ingrid was 10 days? Liz was 11. A competitive urge was coming up in me even in the softest throes of motherhood.

I hadn't time though to really think about running; but I knew that, like most mothers, I would have to go back to work in the end. I knew that eventually I would have to start going away for races and leaving Ciara with Nic. All that was strange to contemplate. The new little person in my life seemed never to be out of my sight once she came home from hospital. The house filled with cards and, apart from a priest back in Leitrim denouncing me from the altar as a slut, it was a perfect time.

I started back in training 10 days after Ciara was born. She was born on the 10th, and on 20 July I laced up my running shoes. I think 10 days was always in my head as the time to make a light start. In the morning I walked down to the river at Teddington and in the evening I went over to the track. Alan Storey and all the gang were there. He said to try a few laps of the track. 'Run off with Lisa there, stay on the track and if you don't feel too good you can stop.'

I'd walked up and I'd brought Ciara with me. She was in the pram and everyone was talking and asking questions, peeping into the pram. Next thing, the group I was supposed to run with were gone. I had to chase after them to keep up, so I was out of breath by the time I caught up. Not a good start. Besides being out of breath, I was stiff and awkward and I felt like I was going from side to side instead of forward. I did 20 minutes, and in the days after I increased it gently so I was doing 23-minute runs for a while, and then I increased it slowly to 28 minutes. Then one day, when my mother was over here, I went with Nic to the park and we met up with a few of the boys from Park Road and I ended up running 40 minutes by accident.

Generally, though, I was very sensible. The day after my first session back, I went to Teddington and met Gerard Hartmann. He sized me up and I ran for 23 minutes with him.

Alan came in to see how things were going. 'You looked a bit awkward when you were running last night,' he said gently.

'How do you mean?'

'Like you were trying not to go to the toilet.'

'You'd feel like that too if you thought your insides were going to fall out.'

'You might not like what I'm going to tell you now . . .'

'Yes?'

'The clothes you have been wearing . . .'

I thought he was going to order me to wear another crop top to stop me bouncing around too much, but he wanted me to wear full tights, a long-sleeved T-shirt and a rain jacket. 'You're running slower and not as far as you'd like, so the more clothes you wear in this hot weather, it will mean that your heart will be working harder and you can run as slow as you need to.'

So soon I was running around in high summer sweating buckets, increasing all the washing I had to do. Things progressed, though. On the Saturday, a fortnight after Ciara's arrival, I ran with Gerard at the track for 28 minutes. He said I looked much better. He was right. It felt very comfortable.

Alan and Gerard held me back a bit when needed. It was on my mind that the Sydney Games were just 14 months away. Soon I was hoping to get in on a proper track session. I said to Alan, 'I want to come to the track and do my second run of the day one Tuesday night soon.' He nodded. I knew that while I was there I was hoping to do a few strides too, but I was half nervous about asking so I decided to play it by ear.

Alan was ahead of me, though. When I showed up he said to me, 'You can run with Robin tonight.'

Well, running with Robin wasn't quite the Olympics, but it was a start. Robin is one of these legendary club runners who come to the track every Tuesday; and so dedicated is he that he owns tracksuits that are coming back into fashion again any day now. He was in his fifties then and wore big glasses all the time. He usually ran with three or four girls. So Alan said, 'Run with Robin, there's nobody with him tonight.' This had been a little joke while I was pregnant: that my first session would be with the women's group and Robin. So I had thought anyway!

I was surprised and excited though to be doing a full track session. I had all the heavy gear on. I was hovering around, trying to get Alan's attention to ask if I could take some of the gear off but I couldn't catch his eye, he was so busy organizing people; so I ended up doing the whole session with all the gear on. Me padded out like Michelin Man. Robin in his big glasses. Lovely.

The return to track sessions was a big step. For the other days, Alan suggested working on the bike in the gym and then coming outside and running for 20 minutes. This was on top of doing 30 minutes' running in the morning. I was running shorter, but running twice a day. I was happy enough with that.

The routine became a run in the morning, then go for a walk with Ciara, and in the evening cycle to the gym (3 miles), do 30 minutes on the indoor bike, run for 20 minutes, and then bike home. And after a while I moved up a group at the Tuesday track session. On Tuesdays at the track there are four groups: the fast group, the second group, and the group called the millennium group – one Tuesday night Alan was watching training and, seeing the biggest group full of golden oldies running around, he suggested that possibly if they were to add all their ages together it would probably add up to a millennium, this being the word thrown around regularly at the end of the '90s. Anyway, I was promoted up to the millennium group for a night. Robin's group is bottom group.

So I warmed up with Robin and told him the news. I was moving up. I felt bad, but Robin was delighted. 'It's good, good that you're progressing up through the groups so quickly.'

Life with Ciara was different in lots of ways. After a morning run I would usually walk with the pram to the track in the evening. One evening I was going to the track, which is about five miles away from home, and I was running late so I jogged through Hampton Court, pushing the pram like a mad thing. I enjoyed it and Ciara seemed to as well. We bombed along, her little face looking up at me, and me chatting to her as we went. It took quite a while for me to realize that the lads from Park Road were jogging along behind us, killing themselves laughing.

We went to a meet at Crystal Palace when she was a few weeks older. I had Ciara in one of those kangaroo pouches and all these people were craning their necks, trying to peek at her. There were doubts as to whether Ciara would last the pace, but I thought she responded well! She had just her feet sticking out and this really funny sun hat on her. People were taking pictures, which didn't really make any difference. Just a sun hat and a pair of feet was all they were getting – but cute anyway.

She slept through most of her first meet, but not all of it. We were standing at the top bend, waiting for the women's 5000 metres to start; the runners were called to the start and, miraculously, this little cry came from the pouch – Ciara was awake. She knew precisely which race to wake up for, which impressed me. I ended up asking for hot water from a man in a chip van to heat a bottle with – not something I ever imagined I'd be doing at a track meet. Nic found us a place, sitting next to John Walker in the stand. They were giving John a presentation and then he was heading on to Zurich. His youngest daughter, Caitlin, was helping me look after Ciara. Every time they fired the starter's gun she nearly jumped out of my lap, so we tried putting our hands over her ears when it was about to go off. I'm not sure which annoyed her more, the gun or the hands over the ears.

It is surprising how easy it is to settle into a new life with an expanded circle of responsibilities. I made up my mind that by the time of the World Championships in Seville I would be back to my regular routine. That way, everyone would be going to the Sydney Olympics in the same shape.

I couldn't ask for more than that!

21

When the calendar flips over and reveals an Olympic year, it makes a bigger and more ominous sound than it does for any other year. It means the start of the countdown. There is a sense of anticipation you get only a few times in your running career. People start asking you questions, and they never stop until the Olympics are in the rear-view mirror.

I remember the New Year's Eve heralding 1996. Atlanta loomed. I was in Dublin, injured and getting treatment with Gerard Hartmann. The New Year flipped over and I felt a distinct sense of tension straight away. It was 1996 . . . Olympic Year. I could feel pressure, this sense of counting down. Pressure. Pressure. Pressure.

For New Year 2000 we were in Melbourne, at home. We didn't travel far on New Year's Eve, we could see the fireworks from the house. The weather grew cool so we watched from the balcony and took in the celebrations in Sydney on the TV. Outside, it was too manic to take Ciara anywhere and the babysitters were looking for small fortunes. A quiet New Year made sense, even if it was an entire millennium that was flipping over.

Lots of people were filled with dread and angst, but it was easier for me. I had dealt with the whole 'getting old' thing on 28 November 1999 when I turned thirty for no very good reason. That had way more of an impact on me than the millennium coming around! In your thirties you automatically get tagged on to words like 'veteran' and 'stalwart' in running magazines. You are well on the way to being an old-timer. Maybe Ciara's arrival gave me perspective, but when 2000 came around I was more relaxed. It felt different, especially as we were in Australia and the Olympic torch was on the way to Sydney, but things were even more different for me. I didn't start the year as I often had, close to full fitness and raring to go. I knew I needed to get down to work and then to take a look at the options for Sydney. Not knowing and not having too much expectation helped ease the pressure.

Early in the year I spent a lot of time talking with Alan Storey, just talking about getting fit again. I was six weeks off race fitness in early January, and that was an optimistic estimate. I was looking towards the middle to end of February before dipping my toe into a race. After that I would be going on a pattern of taking it easy, training hard, taking it easy, and so on. Not all 'eyeballs out', as Alan liked to say. The road to Atlanta had been 'eyeballs out' all the time. So it was easy to convince me. Anyway this is a strange year. The Games are in September. Very late. Normally everyone is winding down by then. This year, that is the target. The summit.

Back in 1999 I had made optimistic plans to have all the Olympic qualifying times wrapped up for myself before Christmas. Then I got a stress reaction in my back before I left London and had to postpone my departure to Australia by a week to get treatment with Gerard in Limerick. It was a nuisance to have to stop running and go back to the drawing board, but there was no choice. Having Ciara had loosened a lot of joints and tendons. Strengthening and repair work had to be done.

I was taking it easy up at Falls Creek before Christmas when I went over on my ankle. Another setback. Another few days off, and my Christmas Day present to myself was the first run out I had been fit for in over a week. I went off on my own and Nic came over and met me with Ciara later. Felt good.

We headed back up to Falls Creek just after the New Year. There was a real Olympic Year buzz about the place by then. We had a nice apartment, Alpine Woodsmoke Lodge. Just myself with Nic and Ciara, with the British marathon runner Richard Nerurkar and a young Craig Mottram as neighbours. There were loads of other athletes in the same block as us. All with Olympic fever. Talking about qualifying times and getting into races here, there and everywhere. All the best Australian middle- and long-distance runners were up there, including Olympic Aussie medal hopefuls Steve Moneghetti and Kerryn McCann. We would be out running and there would be people coming from all angles and at all speeds.

The days in Falls Creek always have their own routine. Once a week we go to the Man, which is the local pub around here (must be short for snowman). We can get good pizza there and play pool for free. The schedule for the rest of the week is more strict: we'd meet at half nine every morning. On Monday, Wednesday and Friday we would drive out about five minutes to Langford's Gap, where good running trails follow the aqueducts that supply the area with water. You can run east or west, it depends on the day. You'd meet those fine, big cows, bred large on all the good air; no kangaroos or koalas, just cows! At the end of the run, we would always go into the dam area of the aqueduct and stand in the ice-cold water in our shorts. Absolutely freezing. The idea was to get the blood flowing to your tired muscles and speed up your recovery from hard training. I'd been at this for a while. I think the idea is that you spend at least 12 minutes in the icy water. At home even, I'd try it with ice cubes added to a cold bath to make sure it was really cold. Anything that is painful has to be good, I figure.

In the evenings at Falls Creek, we'd go out again at 5.30 for a half-hour run around from the village, along more trails that follow another aqueduct. We'd congregate on the top of this hill and do a real easy jog around the place for a half-hour recovery run, followed by another half hour of circuit training and fast strides on return. Then I'd have my own bit of extracurricular work from Gerard to do as well.

I had no firm idea which races I was going to run in the Games. Budapest had been my first experience of the 10,000 metres, and for obvious reasons I hadn't touched one since.

In the medium term, I'd decided to try to run a 10,000-metre race before I left Australia for Europe. Organizers are reluctant to throw very long races into meet schedules, so I didn't want to find myself in the summer wondering when and where I could try to do a 10,000 metres. With the 5000 and the 1500 metres, the same urgency isn't there. I set my sights on the 10,000 at the Australian

National Championships in Sydney on 24 February. If I got under 32.20 there, I would have qualified for the Games. The World Cross Country was down for Vilamoura in Portugal, but I wanted to hedge my bets on that one. Run it if fit enough, otherwise leave it.

We came back to Melbourne with Ciara on 28 January and just kept working away, doing the runs at Fawkner Park and the Tan, plus the regular gym and track sessions. In mid February we headed to Sydney, where the Olympics were already energizing the city. I ran a 5000 metres in 15:10. Leisurely. Headed back to Sydney on the 23rd and had a nice walkabout round the Olympic stadium. It seemed friendlier and more welcoming than Atlanta. I got a good feeling off it. The next night in the 10,000 metres of the Aussie Nationals I ran 31:43 to qualify myself for the Games at that distance if I needed it.

I came back to London in early March and was in Portugal a week later for the World Cross Country. I ran both races. Finished seventh in the 8 kilometres on the Saturday but found it hard to keep up. Tiring stuff in the heat. Then I tried to improve my average on Sunday in the short race, but I came up short, crossing the line in fifteenth position. And the whole weekend was a cause of some friction. Nic wanted me to run both races. Alan wanted me to run only the shorter one. I went with Nic's idea, but maybe Alan proved his point. There would be little conflicts along the way. Everyone was still learning their role in the new set-up around me.

Vilamoura was the real start of the Olympic Year treadmill. Won a 5-mile road race in Balmoral in April. Went back to Milan for the first time since the disaster of 1996 in May, this time for a 10-kilometre road race. In 1996, Milan had finished me, it just put a big punctuation mark at the end of a bad year. In 2000, it made me.

For a start, I knew what I was doing in Milan this time around. I knew what I wanted out of it. I knew why I was there. I aimed for a time of 31 minutes and ducked in a second under, the best I had ever run for a 10 kilometres. What was better was the bonus of beating two great runners like Tegla Loroupe and Derartu Tulu in Milan. Road races are unreliable, but beating two girls of that quality made me feel good. The race came at the end of a hard week when I had clocked well over 100 miles in all.

There was a point in Milan when Tegla left me behind and I caught up to her again and I knew from looking at her that I was feeling so much stronger than she was. At the time Tegla was the best road racer in the world. Sights like that are a tonic. It was an odd race. At one stage Tegla needed to be chased down. Derartu came past me and said, 'C'mon, Sonia, let's go,' as she passed me and chased down Tegla. I was flattered that she believed in me. I wanted to go with her but I couldn't at that stage. My legs just wouldn't. We were on cobblestones at the time and when we got back on to the regular road I was fine again. I could tell that the game was up when I went past Derartu this time and caught Tegla. She just wasn't racing me or responding in any way, so I stayed with her for a while and decided that after 8 kilometres I would go hard again.

On the day before the race an excursion was organized. A viewing of *The Last Supper*. Some nostalgic instinct in me made me decide to go. After all the times I had been in Milan and had never seen anything but track, it just felt right. I didn't know when I'd get the chance to do that again. So I just put our names down for the excursion and off we went. *Last Supper*. I stood in the little room, looking at da Vinci's work, and nothing in my life seemed so big or so bad any more.

That night before the race in Milan we'd had dinner with Derartu. She's a really lovely woman, and her daughter at that time was 21 months old. We swapped motherhood stories. Ciara had come to Milan with us and Derartu made a nice fuss of her. People often ask me about African runners as if there is something intimidating and unbeatable about them. After training and being friends with so many of the guys and girls they have no mystique for me. Later in the day, after the race, I met Derartu in the lift and asked her what she was going to do for the rest of the day. The answer was kind of disappointing and kind of reassuring. She had a coach who sets out her schedule for the time she's away. That evening she was just going out for a short run in the park. No big mystery or secret, just the sort of thing that Alan would have had me doing.

By the time of Milan, I think Alan was beginning to feel reassured about my form. He loves distance running and was keen to help me learn a little more about the 10,000-metre distance. My concentration is brittle and he guessed that for half an hour of racing, with lots of slow laps thrown in, my mind could be anywhere. When I fell behind Derartu and Tegla in Milan, I remember thinking that if I didn't catch up to the pair of them I'd have to train harder. I was musing on this for a while when it struck me that I was way more distracted than I should have been!

Focus was probably the biggest obstacle to me running the 10,000 metres in Sydney. Even though I kept my options open, it was probably inevitable that I would end up running the 5000. All summer, people were playing poker, proving things to one another and concealing things from one another. For me it was different from Atlanta. There was no need for me to be giving shows of strength. I was one of the pack and an elderly lion, not greatly feared any more.

August. Clock ticking louder. I did Oslo. London. Like revisiting old haunts. Oslo provided a strange but personally satisfying outcome. I finished ninth but, for perhaps the first time in a losing race, I came away happy. That was the only unfamiliarity. In Oslo everything seemed the same as when I left, two years ago. They have a new stadium there now, but back then it was the same old charming place and people, year in and year out. The crowds as crazy and as loud as ever.

When you finish ninth you have no idea what you have done, what sort of time you have clocked. I came off the track, pleased with myself – I felt that I had run as hard as I could, but you don't know the detail till you see that time on a screen or a computer printout. When I heard I had done a 4:01 I was surprised. It hadn't felt that fast. I had gone to Oslo with a target time for myself. I was hoping for 4:03, maybe 4:04. My time would have been in the top 10 in the world the previous year. Then again, so would those of the eight girls in front of me!

I ran strongly there and had that feeling runners always have after a good run. I could have run faster. Always you look back and think that if you'd known how strong you'd be in the last 200, you might have gone earlier or pushed yourself to take a second off each of the first two laps.

I used to love pulling away in the Bislett Stadium and the crowd getting to their feet, roaring; but now coming off the track after a blanket finish was a nice experience too. No fuss. No media. A decent time. I sat back and watched the Dream Mile. Then I changed and went back out for another run.

BBC Radio were in the mixed zone. Pretty much the only media that needed me. They asked if they could have a few words. No problem. I thought I'd save on a phone call and tell Alan, my coach, that I'd run 4:01.70 . . .

'As fast as I could go tonight, Alan.'

Naturally, as soon as I got off the air I had to ring Alan to see if he'd heard me being so clever. He was pleased. He'd got into the habit of predicting what I would run in any track race I went to. I had beaten his prediction by three seconds. Oslo marked the end of Alan's career as a soothsayer. It was nice to beat him for once.

London wasn't so happy an experience. I ran a disastrous race at Crystal Palace, just as I had before Atlanta. This time I got dropped after four laps. The Ethiopian, Ayelach Worku, won in the fastest time of the year. I was half a lap and 36 seconds behind her. Way outside my own personal best.

Alan and Nic clashed again afterwards over the amount of work I had done at the track the previous Tuesday. I had done 8000 metres' worth of interval work. Nic felt that the race was a last chance to put down a really good 5000 one last time before Sydney. Alan felt it was all grist to the mill which would get me to the starting line in Sydney in the best shape. Me? I was just unusually relaxed about everything. Having Ciara around put everything into perspective for me. After London I had gone for a run in the park. Alan made a point of coming along with me on the bike. I chatted all the way, and it was only afterwards that it struck me that I hadn't mentioned the Olympics once. Never crossed my mind. Yet that must have been what Alan had ridden along for.

Alan made me cut about 30 miles a week off my training in August. He gave me mileage numbers for the different weeks, and under pain of death I agreed not to exceed them. I had been running a lot without realizing how the miles were totalling up. Now I had a limit. It went against my nature, but in the morning I ran 20 minutes less and in the evening 10 minutes less. I filled in the extra time with stretches and sit-ups and exercises!

Crystal Palace was an echo of the disaster of 1996; then Zurich had its similarities too. I might have asked myself after Crystal Palace why I bothered to run. Zurich answered me each time. I love the place. Funny thing was, there was a point before Zurich when I decided it would be better not to run there at all. I woke up at four o'clock one morning, arguing with myself that I should go. That decided it. I went, and I'm glad I did. In Zurich it was all on the line. I felt I had to do well – and I did. Zurich was my fastest 3000 metres run in a couple of years. Just six days after finding myself threadbare at Crystal Palace, myself and Szabo raced to the death in a 3000 metres in Zurich. She won, but her time of 8:26.36 was by 6 seconds the best for the distance so far in the year. I was a couple of strides behind on 8:27.58. With 150 metres to go I had taken the lead going down the back straight. But Szabo has learned about finishing. She tracked me all the way, and then surprised me by injecting some more pace to go clear as we went into the finishing straight. In Zurich everything was perfect. Before the race I went to the field across from the track and just jogged. I focused on the race and took it easy. The run on the morning of the race is just about going out and getting some air to wake yourself up. Going into London, I felt pressured not to take it too easy, the work I was doing had to be done, I had to look at Sydney. I worked hard. I didn't feel well on the Thursday. In Zurich I got it right.

I had a good win in Gateshead just before I left for Australia, and that was it really, apart from an 800-metre race and a 1500-

metre gallop in Runaway Cove on the Gold Coast of Australia on the Sunday before the Games opened.

The Olympics were so close, I could smell the sweat. We stayed for a while up the coast in Couran Cove, in Ron Clarke's place. We were staying on South Stradbroke Island and half the athletes going to the Games seemed to be living there with us, crowding the runs and the track with all-too-familiar faces. One night we were on the little boat going back to the island, and I turned to see two pale faces sitting like ghosts behind us: Gabriela Szabo and her coach.

Yep, the games are so close that even on the salt air you can smell the sweat.

22

After the heats it is just a countdown. Putting down time. I don't get tetchy. I get less media friendly. I don't have time for the stupid questions. I come off after a heat or I'm going out to a heat and somebody says, 'Sonia, how do you feel?' How do I feel? What do they expect me to answer? I'm going to shout back that I feel dreadful? Nobody'll ever say how they feel if they feel bad. Talking to the press, every athlete feels good. So that kind of thing annoys me. I hide.

We have a house. At Scott Street, in Mortdale, out in the suburbs of Sydney. We are renting, and it is perfect. Close to a necklace of perfect coves and bays. Protected by privet hedge and blessed with a garden for Ciara. And nobody knows we are here. Not even the neighbours. It is so sleepy.

Somewhere in town the Olympics are going on. I take my runs and play with Ciara. When we watch television, we see the Olympics news and the Cathy Freeman news. Cathy is an icon right now. She lit the Olympic flame, a fine and brave thing to distract yourself with, given the pressure she was under. But she is used to distraction by now. In May, after years of working with Nic, she cut him loose months before the Olympics. Her new partner is a Nike executive by the name of Sandy Bodecker. All summer long the Australian media have been taking a cricket bat to Nic and his reputation. As Nic's business partner, Peter Jess, says, 'Bambi has been shot.'

Nic and Cathy get to court before the Games start. The papers are full of stories of Cathy's distress, her hurt on hearing about the arrival of Ciara. Nic is a traitor and a love rat, and about two million other things. I have watched for years the work he has put into Cathy in the middle of a million bitternesses and disappointments and I want to shout it from the rooftops. But I am in a bubble. Nic won't let me be distracted. And it's funny, since he stopped working with her there has been less distraction anyway. I hear little bits and pieces of what is being said in the papers and I catch the odd glimpse. But it is endgame now. It's a painful time but it's necessary. I won't be sorry when it is over, when they are done hacking at each other.

So we live on Scott Street for the Games. I hide.

We get in the big red Land Crawler in Scott Street, me and Nic and Ciara and Alan, and we drive to the Olympic village. I have a little bag. In it I have spikes and number and vest and drinks and shorts and tracksuit. I know because I have checked a thousand times. We drive to the Olympic village. I get a coffee. Read the paper. Find the Irish team manager, Patsy McGonagle, and we catch a bus to the Olympics.

Before the race I go to the warm-up track. Plenty of time. I am there at seven. I race at 8.55. I check in at 8.15. Plenty of time. Always the same story. Before I go jogging, I lie down on my back for 10 minutes and put my legs up in the air. I think about not being nervous. I think about what Alan wants me to do in the race. I concentrate on relaxing. In the distance you can hear the excitement from the huge arched stands. I have been around athletics so long that I can almost tell what each roar and gasp is for. But I fight the distraction and bring myself back to here.

I have 15 minutes tonight, 15 minutes or thereabouts; 15 minutes to find a definition of myself to live with, to find an ending to this obsession, 15 minutes to put a pleasing shape to a career, to justify this lifetime of racing, racing, racing. Fifteen minutes. Maybe less. Hopefully less. One helter-skelter 'eyeballs out' race through Stadium Australia. An Olympic final. Fifteen minutes of gambling on my preparation, on my set of tactics and decisions. It all stacks up pretty high. Think of home. All those tears after Atlanta and Athens and Turin. Here is 15 minutes that will cancel out all those days or add more bitter tears. These are the key pages.

And the key player, Szabo, is here as usual. My ghost. Dominant but not invincible. My theory is, she doesn't like it when there is no rabbit to drag the pace. And Ouaziz, the Moroccan who heads out so fast she might as well be a rabbit, is out with injury. The best Kenyans – Chepchumba, Loroupe and Barsosio – have decided they will concentrate on other distances. I worry about Ayelach Worku, the Ethiopian, about Gete Wami, and about Olga Yegorova, this Russian who appeared from nowhere to win in Stockholm last month.

Fifteen minutes. It's not so much, Andy Warhol.

I don't know why I put my legs in the air. I know I did it before the World Student Games in Sheffield in 1991 and I won, and I've been doing it ever since. There's no reason for it. I just think it's a good thing to do now. Not sure why. I have these superstitions. I think you run faster in white shoes.

I hear a familiar voice pulling me from my thoughts. Not even a voice. Ciara. With my dad. My dad could get in and out of Colditz without breaking sweat. I play with Ciara in the infield till it is time to go. My dad tells me he loves me – but I knew that when he smuggled Ciara in here somehow!

At ten to eight Alan and I walk a lap of the track. He tells me the race will be consistently hard. He tells me to be stubborn. To watch out. To fight. Inside the stadium, Cathy Freeman is racing to a gold medal. They broadcast the whole thing to us out here on the warm-up track. The tannoy is too loud and crackly but the crowd noise tells us the result anyway.

Back to the business of warming up. Sprint. Jog. Stretch.

Is it a computer program that puts together the Olympic schedule? If it is, well, congratulations on building in a sense of humour. Tonight Cathy Freeman and I share the stage. First Cathy Freeman. Then me. Her old nemesis, Mary-Jo Perec, has gone home to France. The stage was set. The stadium has been like a pressure cooker all night long. You can see steam about the place now.

Funny. There are no Chinese here tonight. The great wonders of Ma Junren rolled their eyes and shrugged their shoulders and decided to stay at home instead of appearing in Sydney when they heard about the testing for EPO which was going to be imposed on them. Makes you wonder how much of your career you can make sense of, because you will never know the full story.

Even tonight. What is coursing through the blood of the other girls on the line? You don't want to stop and imagine all the murk there might be out there. You can only race what is put out against you and hope for the best. Sean Kennedy. Kim. Alan. Nic. They have never turned out a dirty athlete. Your reputation is all you bring with you, really. You just hope people trust you.

I don't feel any edginess until the day before the first race when they hand out the heat sheets and give each runner the number they'll wear on their vest. They give you your number the day before so you don't lose it. I get a bit nervous then. They give you the heat sheet too. Like exam results. I'll come out of the room and they'll have the list of all the other runners' names and the year each one was born and their best time for this year and their best time ever. I always look at that list and I always notice the same two things: they all look really great on paper, and I've got the hardest heat!

Funny, the heats were fine and uncomplicated. The last Olympic race I ran was in Atlanta and it was a heat. If I had paused to look back, that might have been something I gave space to in my mind. I didn't. On the day before the heats I just did a 35-minute run in the morning and a 23-minute jog in the evening. In between we went walkabout. We did Ciara things. We went to the shops. If the Olympics were happening, they weren't happening in my head.

On Friday, the day of the heats and a week after the opening ceremony where I carried the Irish flag, I had 23 minutes around Olds Park and then a trip to the Olympic village. I'd got accredited for the Games up in Melbourne but it was easier to get to the stadium going by the village first and getting one of the shuttles.

The heats were slow and not a worry. I ran 15:07 to top the list of qualifiers for the final. That time won't be nearly adequate, come Monday. I reckon on having to run 14:45, maybe faster. Still, there's nothing left but to run the race. There's some good runners to beat, I tell the press folks, but you don't win an Olympic medal any other way. This has to be the race of my life.

Meanwhile I had the weekend to look forward to. Out to lunch the next day with Nic and Ciara. Down to watch the marathon on Sunday. Nobody told me the Games could be like this. Thank God I came to this stadium in February. It feels good, knowing what to expect. Coming from the warm-up track to the main stadium and the tunnel, I've been here a few times now, I know what's around every corner. These final minutes. The whole process can be really irritating. They make the little announcements.

Women's 5000-metre runners, 10 minutes.

Women's 5000-metre runners, 5 minutes.

They get into your head.

The call room is too small. Across the tunnel there is a little bit of track. People wander across and sprint up and down it. You can see the nerves on people's faces.

I bought a book last week. I was out shopping just for some distraction and my eye fell on *Winning Attitudes*, edited by the great Herb Elliott. I brought it home for dipping into when the hours dragged. There were just tons of positive thoughts rounded up and placed between two covers. Perhaps I could borrow one.

I like positive thoughts. When I knew Nic first, he never realized that I needed reassurance with the thoughts I had, going into races. He would talk a lot to his own runners, but he'd reckon that I had everything sussed. I missed that about Kim for a little while; he would tell me I was in the form of my life. And he would tell everyone else, and I would hear it back from people who liked to pretend to know these things. And I would believe it because everybody else did. It took Nic a little while to realize the level of reassurance I need.

It was Nic with gentle nudging who persuaded me towards the 5000 metres at a time when I was starting to look at the longer race. Nic told me that I would be unhappy sitting looking at the 5000 on telly, knowing I should have had a medal. That idea made sense to me and lifted me.

There was a bit in the book about the voice inside you. The voice that says, 'Do you want to do this?' That is precisely the voice which I have been trying to listen to for a couple of years now. And there it was, jumping off the shelf to remind me that it was there. Must mean something.

Then somebody comes to round us up from the warm-up track and lead us to the call room, where we will wait before we go into the stadium. The people who do the lead-in, they walk soooooo slow, like it's a funeral. You want to walk past them to hurry it up, but you know what happens: they call you back like you are a kid. Walk behind me. Single file, please. People get annoyed. It's this slow walk through the tunnel. Sometimes we go into another holding room. Anyway, when you come out the other side and into the stadium and it's all very loud, you find you are irritated and unfocused. Tonight though something funny happens. Szabo just starts jogging. Somebody follows her. And another and another. And the official starts jogging. We are all jogging. It is ridiculous and I am laughing as we burst out into the stadium.

I try to stay as relaxed as I can for as long as I can. Warming up and strides. When they take you to the starting line and put your stuff in the basket and take it away, then a minute starts to seem like a long time. They call your name out in the stadium and always when you hear it, it's like a shock and they stick that camera in your face and you think, what do I do here now? Wave? Smile? Grit my teeth? Sometimes you don't see it there and that's probably when you are most into what you are doing. Usually you give a little wave. Then you crouch and the gun goes off and you forget about it all. Tonight is the same. Just racing.

So bang and off we go. In Atlanta, these moments terrified me. Here in Sydney the very thought of the final has made me happy. And now we are off and into it and I am the happiest runner in the pack and the stadium settles into a hum of noise, waiting for somebody, anybody, to make a move.

By the fourth lap the knife is in. The field shifts forward. I go nowhere. For two laps I am adrift. It wasn't that I suddenly slowed up, everyone else just started going quicker.

And like a charm, the book comes to me: Herb Elliott and Co.

I have to answer that question. Do I want this? I have to look at the shoulder blades and elbows ahead of me and ask it, not for the first time: do I want this? It's easy to say yes when you are on the training track or with Alan, but not here in this strange, lonely place, on your own in front of a packed stadium and with half the world watching. Cos if you want this you have to give every ounce that you have and you have to understand that you might fail. I ask myself the question. Yes. I give myself up to the race. It might break me before I break it.

I don't know how I get around tonight. Am I focused? It feels like one of those races in which I am just not thinking about anything. My mind is completely free, completely blank. I hang in behind Jo Pavey of Britain. Just stay with Jo. I am back in the race after a while. The pace slowed and for a while it was carrying me along. Now I am between two Kenyans, then I am dragged along by the Ethiopians. I don't know what is going on with them. They are arguing. Wami is shouting at the other two. There are elbows flying in here. Wami wants to go but can't get free. I'm just with them as they argue.

Suddenly I realize this is a race, we are flat out. The stadium is electrified. The tempo keeps getting pumped up. I don't think I can go any faster, but I am so pumped and excited I can't go slower either. My lungs will burst at any second. More Sonia drama for the papers.

These last four laps are a bit of a dream. I haven't been this far inside the heart of a race for a long, long time. I have this feeling that the race is running us. We have no idea how fast we are going. The crowd are a blur. We exist only relative to one another. I wait. Wami waits. Szabo waits. Flying around but waiting. Our strange job.

Down the back straight, Irina Mikitenko from Germany comes from nowhere. She isn't supposed to win. Szabo and I go after her. Hey! We haul her back. Now it's the two of us. No idea about the land behind. Just the bend and the home straight left.

Szabo goes first. She knows I am about to pull the trigger. She outdraws me. But now I am gone too. She has the inside lane and she is clever. As we come off the bend, her elbows do this odd wide shuffle; it makes it seem as if she is going even faster. It distracts me for a second.

We do these last 200 metres flat out in 28 seconds. Scorching the earth, running on air. It is as exciting and as pure a race as I have ever known. Gabriela Szabo makes it to the line ahead of me. Her arms stretch out wide. My head looks towards the heavens.

Happy or sad? I am a person who hates to lose, but tonight I know the truth of it when they say that at the end of the day you are competing against yourself, getting the most out of yourself. Szabo and I threw it all down on the track tonight. Every ounce. She won, but I was coming from a place so far back, from Atlanta and Athens and Turin and every circle of racing hell, that I don't feel as if I lost. This was the most I could give. At the time and in the place I most needed to give it.

Nic and Ciara are here suddenly. They knot themselves around me. Happy. Happy. Happy.

I take a lap of honour just as Cathy Freeman is getting her medal. Her nation's flag is raised as I sprint down the straight with a furry wombat in one hand and a tricolour in the other. Happy. Happy. Happy.

As a postscript to my Games, I can't resist the 10,000 metres. The final gets away from me early though, and I am stranded in sixth place. And the funny thing is, there is no tragedy. I don't feel it. I hear voices from the crowd, Irish voices pushing me on. So I go on. Lap after lap. In sixth spot. Hopelessly adrift but this is my final. I find a rhythm and I go faster than I have done for this distance before.

It's strange to be out here. Alone almost, with just the rhythm of my own footsteps to bring me along, but that's where it started in Cobh many years ago. Me and my footfall. I keep going. Keep moving. I have a silver medal. I have the love back in my heart. This is all good. This is the dreamtime.

23

In Sydney, Kim was there but he wasn't very much a part of the Olympics for me. When I look back I don't even know where he stayed while we were there. We had our own house and our own routine. By the time the race came about, it was like we were living there in Sydney rather than visiting the Olympics. What presence Kim had was on the mobile phone, an invention which seemed to suit him. I remember speaking to him on the phone amid the chaos of the following morning, out in Scott Street with TV crews and reporters starting to call.

In the couple of years after 1998 Kim and I spent very little time together. He had little or nothing to do with my training. I did everything with Alan Storey's group. Nic looked after a lot of things. It's true that we were in Marrakech together for the World Cross Country Championships; and at the 1998 Euro Championships in Budapest, Kim was there all the time too. We even went back to the old thing of running back to the hotel after the track meet ended. He organized the best of everything always. From the end of 1998 though, and on through 1999, I wasn't around much; I was pregnant with Ciara and I had bits and pieces of injuries.

In 2001, before Sophie, my second girl, was born, I tried the World Indoor Championships in March. I finished seventh in the 3000 metres and ninth in the 1500 metres and then started to wind down for Sophie's arrival. Kim and I started to talk a lot more again. It was just one of those things; enough water had gone under the bridge and we began talking about different things. I started to enjoy his company again as a friend and somebody whom I knew I would get a straight answer from if I had a question to ask. If there was something I wasn't sure about, I could call him and ask, and I knew I would always get an answer, some words that would influence me.

In 2001 the Goodwill Games were in Australia. So too was the Grand Prix final. Athletics was trying to suck the last of the good feelings from Sydney out of the Australian public. Anyway, it made sense for us to go down to Australia quite early, at the end of August, rather than just before Christmas.

It had been a good year, following on from the Sydney Games.

I met with Kim a few times in Melbourne. It was always in the back of my mind to get him more involved and more hands-on with my career again, now that we were at ease with each other. I had this nagging feeling in my head that maybe I should ask Kim to coach me again, to have a bigger influence on what I was doing in some way. I don't know why. I felt I was missing something. I could run well, run fast, win some races; but I had lost the invincibility thing. I thought maybe Kim could get that back for me. That iron belief he had in things. I hoped it was still contagious.

So the question just sat in my mind like a parcel in the hallway waiting to be posted. I was going to ask him the year before, Olympic Year, but after the buzz of Sydney the need to talk about my career receded a bit. So many times it was there on the tip of my tongue just to ask, but it was a big question and I dreaded getting knocked back.

Anyway, during this time in Melbourne I was comfortable. Since the first trip to the city in 1995 I had been going to this place called The Bakery on Domain Road beside the Tan. Now that we had plenty of time to put down in Melbourne, Kim would meet me there for coffee some mornings.

We sat outside one day, chatting, and it was killing me to ask him. I don't know why I was nervous or scared but, even though the idea was strictly career-related, it felt like a marriage proposal. We had got back to this really good relationship and I was at a stage again when I could use some good positive energy from Kim and I didn't want to wreck it all, all the years of growing close again. I didn't want to throw all that rehabilitation between us away with one question.

Eventually I blurted it out. 'Kim,' I said, 'I've been trying to ask you this question for months. Would you consider coaching me again?'

He was stunned. He couldn't believe it. It wasn't often that you would see Kim McDonald surprised by something. I looked at his face. He was surprised and pleased.

He said he would love to.

That was the last proper conversation we had.

We were in Brisbane just after that for the Goodwill Games and then we came back to Melbourne. Kim had remained in Brisbane on a holiday and, typical of Kim, he was vowing to do loads of cycling and stuff. He was on one of his drives where he would start pushing the barriers to get fit. Kim was always a man of extremes, either really fit or totally unfit, either doing masses of exercise or doing nothing at all. There was no in-between, nothing middle of the road.

I was in Noosa. He was in Brisbane. We were in touch through texts and the odd call. Kim told me one day that he was going for a bike ride on the Sunday. There was the annual Noosa Bolt, a 5-kilometre road race going on up in Noosa, and he was torn. He was kinda thinking of coming up to Noosa for the race, but he wanted to go bike riding. He sent me a message asking me to just send him the result of the race. There was never a race that Kim wasn't interested in the results and times.

There were two or three text messages back and forth. The last one was 'thanks'. I went from Noosa to Melbourne. Kim was coming the following week. I sent him a text, asking him to let me know when he got to Melbourne. I heard nothing back, but that wasn't unusual.

I was in touch with Kim on Saturday after the 5-kilometre road race. I went back to Melbourne on the Sunday and sent Kim another text that day. He died that Sunday.

It was really eerie. I knew Kim was going for a bike ride. I just didn't know much more, but pretty early on I got a strange feeling about it. I got my sister Gillian who lives in Brisbane to call this bike shop in the city. She found out where Kim would have been riding from. I got the number and called them. I asked them if he had been on the bike ride. He hadn't. The guys knew that Kim had been expected.

I had started making more calls when one of my friends who was living in Australia at the time, a girl called Tina Ryan, phoned and told me. I can't remember how she had found out about Kim's death. He was by himself in his hotel room. They said it was a heart attack. All alone.

I wasn't allowed to travel for Kim's funeral; Sophie was imminent by then. But Kim left a space in all the lives of those who shared his mad passion for running, so many people he coached and encouraged and managed. All the great Kenyan athletes he brought from poverty in the Rift Valley to superstardom on the tracks of Europe and America. And me. He was good and honest and scrupulous with his athletes and he wanted the best for all of us.

Our time together was a shared obsession, almost a madness. In the end, during that time in Australia, I don't think Kim loved me in that kind of boy/girl way; but by then, no matter how hurt he had been, he always cared a lot for me and would always have helped me.

There were times, because of what he was involved in, when Kim's life seemed like an endless series of distractions. He handled it, but he was always under pressure. Kim would be talking to at least fifty people a day. He wouldn't have much time to think or reflect, but when the running season was over he would have a lot more time for lunch or for dinner, and he was always good company.

In 1998, in the months before Ciara was born, Kim had this girlfriend, Brenda, from New Zealand. I became really good friends with her. We'd go to the gym together all the time. When you aren't training seriously you need somebody to go to the gym with. We used to run together. It was good. Felt normal. I was happy that Kim had somebody else, not that I would ever be worried about anything like that from him. There was a line and there would be no crossing it. He was a man who saw everything, except people, in black and white. He was a very unusual person.

When I ended our relationship, he just accepted it. He never tried to get us back together, never used his influence as he could have. Never even spoke about it. There was no return.

I had thought about it for a long time myself, procrastinating. I suppose our split was coming for a long time before 1996. You get to a point when you have to stand still and stay the way you are because it is the Olympics that is coming over the horizon, and if you have to change things you are in trouble. I depended on him for training, racing, organizing my whole life and putting everything in place. He had taught me a lot of stuff, from the time I first went to London. I remember the first time I saw his apartment. It was so sterile clean, everything had to be a certain way, the books were in their special positions, just so on the table, and if somebody moved them he would know. If you moved them an inch he would know. He was just so neat with everything. I was quite young and all over the place. I picked up things like that.

I feel that how I am now, well, a lot of it was influenced by the way Kim was. My neatness started with seeing that apartment. I'm not obsessive to that extreme but if I leave the house now, everything has to be put away before I go. I can't leave dishes in a sink. I can't leave them on the draining board. I have to dry them and put them away. I have to fold all the clothes. I have to put them all away properly. Everything has to be done in a particular way.

More than a bit of Kim's obsessiveness rubbed off. It makes me hard to live with, and makes it difficult at home for Nic sometimes. Nic will do household things just fine, but for me they won't be done the right way. I come in, maybe from an airport, maybe from training, and straight away I am doing the things my way even if Nic has done them already. I'll come in and clean the sink. I have to try really hard not to say anything negative about Nic's sink cleaning. I'll come in the door and I'll be scrubbing away and Nic will come through and ask me what I am doing. He can't understand. By doing it myself it's not like I am complaining. I just have to do it my way. It has to be so white. I am annoying, I know it! I can't come back from a long trip without unpacking everything and leaving shorts and T-shirt at the end of the bed for the next morning's run. Totally loopy. Even these days, when I can only make it for a jog. I blame Kim!

Kim was always one of those people who, when he was around, you knew he was on your side, all of us who ran for him. You just felt really good. Over the years he gathered a lot of other people around him and there was always this positive energy, this sense that nothing was impossible; and it helped you to believe in yourself more than anything else. At a meeting, Kim would be out there, not just telling you how well you were going but telling everybody else. Soon the place would be buzzing that I was going to do this, that or the other. When that went, so too did the sense that people were afraid of me.

All the parts of my life, the fourth places, the silver medals, the disasters and the tears, they were all part of the road to somewhere. I don't know if I would swap anything for the happiness I have now with Nic and Ciara and Sophie. Kim was part of that pathway and it is hard for everyone who knew him to see his enthusiasm gone from our lives.

24

How do you wind down a career as an athlete in a way that makes you happy? If you are a footballer or a hurler, they move you to different positions, you play fewer matches, you come on as a substitute, you manage your training differently. As a runner, you just fade away.

Since Sydney, since Kim passed, there have been good days and disappointments, but the real world crowds in; for instance, I remember the World Cross Country in Dublin in 2002 with a special fondness. Our team, myself, Ann Keenan-Buckley, Rosemary Ryan, Valerie Vaughan, Maria McCambridge and Maureen Harrington, came third in the team event. A bronze medal. I literally jumped in the air for joy when I was told we had secured the bronze. I had one from Turin, of course, but on that day in Turin I was so wrapped up in my own woes I didn't take from it what I should have. For the three of us, at home in Ireland in 2002, it was a special day. I had my two daughters with me in Leopardstown, and Sophie was just three months old. It still gives me a kick to have come back to seventh place in the individual race that afternoon, 12 weeks after she was born.

Going up that hill on the racecourse for the third time that afternoon was tough. What kept me going was the other girls on the team and the fact that I was dying to get to sixth place because I'd been seventh twice before. I enjoyed it, though. That may seem an obvious thing to say, but when you've been away you tend to enjoy it more when you come back; and you fear you may have forgotten how to dig in that little bit more until you hurt yourself!

That summer I traded in my two European Championship golds from Budapest for a pair of silvers in Munich. I ran an Irish record time of 30:47.59, to come second in the 10,000 metres behind

Paula Radcliffe. Paula set a brilliant European record in the process that day, knocking on the door of 30 minutes. A few days later, I made a silly tactical error which cost me the gold in the 5000 metres. Slow learner! Shortly afterwards though, I went to my favourite stamping ground in Zurich, and in coming third I set my season's best for the 3000 metres, a time of 8:33.62. Not too shabby for a 33-year-old mother of two.

Later in 2002 I struck out on another adventure: my first serious marathon. New York. I'm not sure I got it right nor am I sure now that the distance is for me. To prepare, I did a lot of long runs with the Australians who were still hanging on to the end of the track season, including Benita Johnson and Craig Mottram, who had just started to really listen to Nic after some dismal results at the Commonwealth Games in Manchester. Nic often came with us on the bike and, with the speedometer in place, he was able to let us know how far and how fast we were going when we needed to be reminded to go faster or slower; he would try to dictate the pace from the bike. All summer my times weren't just good, they were astonishing. Finally I decided there had to be something wrong with the speedometer on the bike. If there was, though, it was too late to do anything about it.

Anyway, as the race approached, Ciara went back to nursery school and Nic decided it would be a nice idea if he had a baby seat welded to the back of the bike; that way, baby Sophie could come along for the rides through the park. So the mountain bike went in to have a seat attached and, when it came back, all my times were much slower.

I called the bike shop.

'Did you do anything to the speedometer?'

'Nope.'

So I don't know if it was measuring too short, or was it measuring too long? I just decided I didn't care and would continue running the routes I had my landmarks on all summer.

I enjoyed New York as an experience, but the race itself fell apart on me. In training, I had been running on course for anything between 2:20 and 2:25. On the day, I got into trouble going along the Queensboro Bridge and came home in twelfth place with a modest time of 2:32:06. The winner, Joyce Chepchumba of Kenya, was six minutes ahead of me. Where I had planned to be.

As you get older, it gets harder to be where you had planned to be. At the 2003 World Championships in Paris I ran a fine heat and a disastrous final. That's the way life goes.

The following year I dithered for the longest time over going to the Athens Olympic Games. First, things would go well, then they would go badly. I remember a crisis when I was running in Madrid. I was just wondering if I had the will, wondering if I was still answering yes to that question, do I want this? The track in Madrid is in Canillejas, out in the suburbs. I was set up to run well. Nic asked for a fast pacemaker to haul me along. Yet it was a night when nothing could make me go faster, and I knew after 200 metres that I was wrong. But by then I was committed to Athens and there was less drama about going than about not going. So I went.

Yet on a night like that, in a half-empty stadium, coming home to twelfth place, it was just hard to believe that once upon a time I had done this all the time. And I used to do it well. But life was different now. Twelfth place left my head full of doubts again, but Sophie and Ciara had come out to Canillejas, not to see their mammy race but to see the fireworks, so that is what we had to do. No brooding runs back to the hotel. Life went on. We watched Roman candles and Catherine wheels and parachute shells and firepots fizzing and banging in the sky. The girls looked on in wonder. Their faces cheered me up. It was their time. That's life now.

Somewhere along the line I stopped having the energy that goes with being wide-eyed and innocent, and I started chiselling a late career out of my experience. In recent years, when going into a race, I would have to have not just Plan B but sometimes even a Plan C. Sometimes that Plan C is just to not think about the race again once it finishes!

The Games? A few times I thought about just not going. More

than a few, I suppose. But that night in Madrid (funnily enough, maybe for the first time, to be honest) I wasn't thinking strongly about not going. I had done enough to have every reason to go. I looked at getting into the final and I hoped that anything might happen after that. Could Athens beat Sydney as an experience? Could anything I might achieve in my fourth Olympics add to the legacy of the last dozen years? In my heart I knew the answer was probably 'no'.

It was strange, dipping into the circuit again on the way to Athens. All those years ago I was top dog. In 2004 I showed up a few times in hotels where the circus had pulled in for Grand Prix action, and I walked among them like a ghost. Yeah, I used to be Sonia O'Sullivan! I'd walk into a hotel, with them all there, and not even know who was who. I'd talk to managers and coaches and agents because they had been there forever! Races stopped meaning so much, perhaps when I realized that to me they meant too much and losing them was killing me. Or maybe when I realized that what to me was a part of my personality was just entertainment for the rest of the world, not life and death.

I lost a race in Gateshead earlier in the year. I had set my heart on winning it. I headed back to London thinking that, this being England and everything, so many people would have seen me lose: neighbours and the parents of Ciara's and Sophie's friends. People who run in the park. People in local shops. I'd go home and they'd have seen my day's work on television and shaken their heads in pity and sadness. But people were nice. Interested. They were telling me that I don't normally run the 1500 much any more.

Nic found it harder. Sometimes we would have to talk about athletics. It can be claustrophobic though, and I try to block it out. It's harder for him because he doesn't understand why I've decided to do what I've decided to do in a race or training session. He doesn't know why I've decided to behave that way. Because I want to move on and forget about it, I refuse to discuss it. With his other athletes he's a talker. They talk about everything. They get to the bottom of a problem and figure it out. That doesn't happen with me. There is no bottom, so if we can't get to the bottom of it we might as well leave it and move on.

I suppose the memory of Athens that I will always carry is that last lap. Looking back now, I am glad I went to Athens. At the time I didn't really enjoy it or appreciate it for what it was, but I think I was fit enough to justify being there. I was a bit unlucky not to have the chance to show that fitness on the day because I know that, without being so sick and weak from a bout of food poisoning and the lack of fuel in my body, I could have been in the mix at the end of the race. I know this because I ran so well after the Olympics. I had to accept that I didn't get it right on the day, but I deserved to be there so I had to take my chances.

I had reached the 5000-metre final, hoping that anything could happen. It did. Again! I was feeling heavy-legged and sick and I came home last in a field of 14, well over a lap behind Meseret Defar, who took the gold.

But on that lap something happened, people just started clapping me and I started waving back. There, in the stadium that had nearly broken me in 1997, I was given almost a hero's reception by the crowd as I jogged around my last lap. It was so poignant and lovely. The way to say goodbye.

I had felt so slow and hopeless out there. It was with about four laps to go that I realized I was all alone, circling the track behind a race that I was watching on the big screen. Then I also noticed the Irish flags on the top bend; they hadn't been there at the start of the race, they must've moved down close to the track to be closer to me, to share my pain. It all just turned from pain and tears of hopelessness to tears of emotion at what those Irish supporters were doing for me. They were carrying me closer to the finish, and I went from looking for a hole in the track to disappear into to getting a little bit of hope, a light at the end of the tunnel. There was the finish line, I was getting closer to it; and there were some people who would go home in sadness, not joy, but they were sticking with me to the end. So I had to stick with them and get to the finish line with a wave of thanks as I circled an Olympic track for the last time! Not the ending I had dreamed of, but a nice one to write on the spur of the moment.

You can't change things. You can't unring a bell. That was how it was supposed to end.

25

When I watch the girls in the garden, running around in the sun, all brown-limbed and happy, I ask myself the question that a lot of people ask me. Would I like them to be athletes? Would I like them to do what I did?

'Not really,' is the answer. In a funny way I'd like them to play something different, like tennis or maybe golf; any game that would put them in the mix with people. I don't know that I would like them to play a sport which would take over their lives so completely that they would not be able or allowed to do anything else. I'm not sure if I would like them to be involved in sport to the extreme that I am.

Another question. If Ciara or Sophie came home from an Olympics with a gold medal in her pocket and told me she had won it while on drugs, what would I do? I don't know if I could cope. I hate dishonesty; I couldn't handle it. Nic always says that people ask him about athletes and how would you know if they were cheating. You really wouldn't know. People always expect the coach to know. Or a parent would know. Unless the coach is given the results of all the private tests that a cheat does, the coach is just going to think he's being a great coach.

That is the problem the sport I love is left with. You either trust somebody or you don't. If you are honest and open in everything you do, maybe you will be trusted. If you are dishonest or sneaky about things, there is a chance you will cheat. Certain countries have a culture where losing is unacceptable and cheating is toler-ated. It is a mystery to me, but when I look at people who get caught I often think this: if I ever took drugs and got caught, I could never go home again, never look my mam and dad in the eye, or John Treacy or Marcus or Frank or Nic.

Nobody I have ever trained with ever tested positive. Nobody

Kim ever trained with. Or Alan. Or Nic. That has to be what you stand for.

I go on the Internet sometimes and I see people being questioned on websites, people who can't see why the improvements are there. I am amazed at the way the atmosphere surrounding athletics has changed. When any runner is quite good, there is an easy accusation to be made. That's our tragedy in what is the simplest, purest sport: racing to see who can run the quickest.

There are people cheating just to hang on in the circuit. There are pacemakers who cheat just to stay on as pacemakers.

I am an idealist. People often ask me about great runners, just as I am sure people have asked others about me. They ask me, say, about Haile Gebrselassie. I say that I can't see it. If Haile was ever to test positive, it would be a disaster. The Kenyans and Ethiopians are different from us. They have a built-in facility. They are beatable at the end of season. It runs out. They get tired. They are away from altitude. I can explain Haile's brilliance.

Marion Jones has been a disaster for our sport. In a way, I was surprised she was caught. I really wouldn't have thought she was cheating. That is how innocent I am about the thing. To me, she was so much better and she had that shape, bigger and quicker, so of course I thought she would win because she is built to win. It is hard to understand the whole drug test thing. I've never been to any of these big conferences. I wonder what goes on there. Do they present this whole ideal situation and then can't live up to it? There seems to be a lot of wastage.

When I am at the Olympics, do I believe in the sprint events any more? To be honest, not across the board. Too many people are testing positive. Other people are taking as much as they can that is legal. One bottle here. Another bottle there. The difference is some abstract rule. I find it hard to believe any more.

The throwing events? The throwing at Olympics and World Championships is often more realistic than for the years in between. You get a more level playing field there because the testing has cleaned up this area of the sport. Most of the throwing records that exist would have to be questioned.

The problem is, people you like and feel comfortable around, you never want to suspect. People you don't know, other cliques, they must be the drug problem that everyone is talking about.

There are some: Kim Collins won the 100 metres in Paris in 2003. He was a skinny guy, a nice guy. You think, ah, if he can win, maybe they aren't all cheating.

It disillusions me a bit. This Balco stuff and everything. You think, why bother? Everyone's cheating. It's boring to have to read about it or listen to it; what they are doing, who is doing it. That's not what you run for. When I see what I do and what Benita Johnson and Craig Mottram, my friends and training partners, do; when I look at the hard work and the care and the detail that goes into it, I get queasy. I wonder then what percentage are cheating, what percentage aren't. The cheats? Are they laughing at us? I suppose they must be. You can't think too much about it. You have to close it off and get on with it.

People make the point to me that, from Barcelona onwards, they can find cheats in my races; when they subtract them from the equation, I should have got this medal and that medal. Even Gabriela Szabo had her controversy. In 2003 a car belonging to her was pulled in and found to have EPO in its boot. She denied all knowledge, but her career was a bit up-and-down after that.

It's not for me to wonder any more. I never really thought of Gabriela Szabo in that way because she never ran or achieved anything that I believed I couldn't match. She had a couple of dominant years, and I had the same. But did she do things she shouldn't have been able to do? I don't know. If she beat me, I never thought it was the worst disaster ever because, whatever was going on with her, I knew I could beat her on my day. The Chinese phenomenon was the worst ever. Just the way they came and went. I hated never getting another chance at racing against them.

What's worst for me isn't the rumours and the what-might-have-beens that eat your energy up. It is when people get caught cheating and either they get banned or they go away for a while . . . and then they come back. Brazen. No different. They seem to have no conscience. I walk into a hotel and feel embarrassed because I've been away for a while, having a baby. They'll walk into a hotel after a ban for cheating everyone else and they never feel any remorse or embarrassment.

All that, it makes me miss the world of athletics less. It is easier to move on because of it.

26

I became an Australian citizen just before the Commonwealth Games in 2006. The usual controversy! I often look at Catherina McKiernan and wonder how she manages to stay out of the limelight or why I manage always to put myself in it. There must be a happy medium somewhere between us.

Anyway, I didn't deprive any Aussie of a spot on the team. I earned my spot and then got injured anyway, so I never ran. There was no negative reaction towards me in Australia, but I think there was a lot of confusion at home. All Dublin taxi-drivers for instance assume I have just arrived from Australia any time I come in at the airport, and they assume I am on my way back to Australia any time I go to the airport. I don't live in Australia any more than I used to. We split our time between London and Melbourne, due to the work commitments of Nic and myself.

When I am in Australia I am always a lot more relaxed, it is like I am on a long holiday . . . so I get to run lots and get really fit, then when I come back to London I seem to have lots more to do. As London is so close to Ireland, I can go home at the drop of a hat and I sometimes think I spend my life driving back and forth to Heathrow. The car could get there on autopilot.

I love it when I spend time in Ireland, though it is more often Dublin for work or Limerick for physio; but we go to Cobh with Ciara and Sophie at least once in the year.

I took Australian citizenship (and still have Irish citizenship) not just for the Commonwealth Games but for Nic and Ciara and Sophie. It makes things easier in terms of having the choice of staying in Australia for as long as I want to, not as long as I am allowed to, and it is nice to share some of their identity and that of a country which has been so good to me.

In my head I am still Sonia from Cobh, though. I am not quite ready to be anything else. If I support Australian athletes in sport for instance, it is more for Ciara and Sophie; they are big into supporting Australia and wearing their Socceroos jerseys around the place. I haven't learned to consider myself Australian yet. Any time I come to Ireland and people assume I live in Australia, I am a little disappointed. I am not ready for that.

I didn't make the decision to be an Australian. I needed it and wanted it and I did everything I could to get to get the passport. I am glad that I have an Australian passport and I would like to keep it, but I was born and raised in Cobh. I will always be Irish. The Aussie citizenship ceremony was nice though, like another event in your life, a bit of a landmark. It's a real big deal and I got mine at the last minute, so I didn't know much about the protocol until the morning of the ceremony.

I thought I had taken all the tests, filled in all the forms, counted all the days in order to be granted citizenship at one time. Then they said, 'No, you don't actually.' It all gets very technical when the days are added up, and the time I spent in Australia training and racing didn't add up to the required number in the right order. I was really surprised when I walked in to meet the top people at the Department of Immigration in Melbourne, expecting my papers to be all stamped and be handed the passport, only to be told the numbers didn't add up. I was so disappointed, the excitement and anticipation just flooded out of me. I felt so let down and annoyed with myself. It turned out that the only way for me to get citizenship was if we got married. So we did. Happily.

The bad news dropped on me just as I was about to get on a plane back to Ireland to do some work with Supervalu. I was in Ireland for 10 days in January. Nic had to organize everything. I came back and we went straight to Falls Creek. I got picked up off the plane at five in the morning. We were in Falls Creek for about two weeks, then we got married on 25 January 2006.

There was nobody there. Very small gathering. I told nobody. Just me, Nic, Ciara and Sophie, and Peter Jess and Garry Henry. I didn't want a big deal. We needed a couple of witnesses, so Peter and Garry fitted the bill perfectly. Garry is a long-time friend of

Nic's whom I have known since 1996, and he is now also part of our training group, riding the bike every day with the athletes wherever they are in the world. Peter is renowned for turning up at all big sporting occasions, and it was he who gave me 'Fatso', the controversial wombat, as I went to collect my silver medal in Sydney.

Ciara and Sophie wore the dresses they had been given for Christmas and they had these nice sandals, or so I thought. We came out of the house and went by train into the city. Walking down the road to Richmond train station, Sophie's shoes were no good, she decided. We had to go back and change them. It was a perfect Australian summer's day. We took the train to the city. Went for coffee and muffins. Peter Jess went and got some flowers in the flower shop while we ate. We got married and then went out for lunch.

The next day was the citizenship ceremony. At lunch we had champagne and wine – just sips! Then we all came back and went into the pool. A newspaper guy came over to take my pic. I went across to the MCG park for photos that had me lying on an Aussie flag. Came back from that and went for a run. Two days in a row we had to get dressed up! A run was welcome.

I was always very clear that this was a positive thing and that it wasn't making me less Irish. As it turned out, I never ran for Australia. I got the time and came second in the qualifying race. They didn't want to pick me. Phone calls and all the rest. It was such a big deal about picking me, and in the end I was injured.

Don't know what winning would have been like. Standing there with the Australian flag going up and 'Advance Australia Fair' playing. For the kids, I would have liked it. Sophie is very definite that she is Australian, Ciara not so sure where she stands. Sophie likes to correct her and say, 'No, Ciara, you are not Australian, you are from England.' Sophie is very determined that she is from Australia. She was born there. Ciara was born in England. Strangely, though, Sophie is more Australian in the way she does things. Even when she first spoke, she sounded more Australian than Ciara ever does.

I have reached an age (and so have Sophie and Ciara) when I have to decide where we will live. Since I was 17 I have been moving non-stop. I love Australia but I am not yet sure about living there. I am happier to go down there for a few months at a time. I look forward to it. I am very up in the air about what to do. I go down there. I get into it. I live it. Last year I didn't want to go back, though. Friends in Australia would say, 'What are you looking forward to going back to Europe to?' I didn't really have anything except the obvious. It is home, where I am from, where Mam and Dad live.

Since I was 17 I have been moving all the time. Next thing, next thing, next thing. Afraid to stop. If I am somewhere, there has to be a purpose in being there; if there is no purpose I am unsure of myself. I always had a purpose in training and racing and something I was getting ready for. If I don't have that sense of being busy, I think too much.

Meanwhile, time keeps lapping me. I am 38 writing this. I will be 39 soon. I have to find something to do for the rest of my life. I haven't had the feeling for a long time that you get when you stand on the start line and believe you will win. So life has to be about things outside of running.

I regret some of the things I missed: I missed out on being a part of the Irish team as much as I could have been. That was so visible this past year, watching them work together in Osaka to achieve the best results as a team. When I was there I was at the opposite extreme from the others. The team were happy to qualify. I wasn't happy unless I won. I felt I couldn't be in with everyone else, I would be distracted. I spent a lot of time by myself, doing my own little thing. I didn't have that many friends. I would have loved to get to know better the people on the Irish teams. I watch Irish teams in soccer and lately rugby, and they are so tight with each other. I always felt people didn't talk to me because they were afraid to talk to me. And that was my fault. I know I could have tried a bit harder. I was lucky at the start. I didn't have to try, I fitted in with Frank and Marcus and I was their kid sister. I never bothered about anybody else. When they went, that area of my life stayed empty. I had been like that since I was in school: happier running around the track than getting ready to go to the disco. I got a better feeling, going out to run a race, than going out with friends. It is only now that I know what I missed.

For a long time I cut myself off from all those needs. That was the time, when I was the best as a runner and at my most selfish as a person, I could have taken advantage of the world. I look back and wonder if I couldn't just have enjoyed it more. I try now to do stuff for Athletics Ireland. I finally said to them that I feel a bit isolated because they never ask me to do anything. I spoke to a friend at McDonald's with whom I have been working on a few projects to encourage children to be fit and healthy. She spoke to them too. Athletics Ireland said that I didn't live in Ireland so they never asked me. They were quickly told that, if I lived in Cork, they would have to bring me to Dublin, and that it was just as quick from Heathrow. So they brought me over to do a talk and a clinic at Santry Stadium. That was the start. I loved it.

I don't know where it ends. How it ends, this story. When I have a nagging pain or ache these days and I am bothering Gerard about it, there is a voice asking me why don't I just leave it.

For a while I thought I would find a career in marathons. Even marathons, though, I'm not sure I want to start, knowing I'm an also-ran. I ran in Berlin and got tricked into joining that elite start line. When you are there and you realize you haven't got it, it's hard and lonely just keeping up. Physically, I know I am not in the elite group. Mentally, I'm into in the 'fitness and fun runner' groups. Reconciling that is a challenge. For now, people who are running marathons in fancy dress don't go past me. I was training the other day and there was a man dressed as Batman in the park. It struck me that maybe it won't be too long before I am in races where Batman and assorted teddy bears and mascots are passing me by.

Now it is such a big event for me to run twice in the day. If Nic is away, I can get out once. Hardly ever twice. I can't imagine now a time when running twice a day was just the norm. I'm involved with the kids, I have a normal life. How will it fit in? If

I run twice a day, I end up chasing my tail. In the past couple of years, when I have made the effort to run twice a day it hasn't made a difference anyway. I'm just running to stand still.

Still, I daydream about marathons. Going there low key to enjoy one – and then my head runs away and I'm thinking I'll go somewhere, run a marathon and suddenly from amid the Batman outfits and the Supermen I'd burst away and catch the elite.

It's in the blood, the madness of it.

The good days, I notice, come back to me more readily than the bad. Some things still stir me though. Years and years on, it is still emotional for me to talk about Atlanta; I don't know why. I don't think of Atlanta in terms of two gold medals lost. In some ways I think I am happier with the way things turned out, but it was burned into me as an experience. I watched it all on DVD for the first time recently. It was so strange to watch it all, hard to believe that it was all that long ago and to think of all the things that have happened to me since then.

It was just a moment in time when something didn't work out. It was my moment, but I often wonder, if it had worked out, what sort of person I would have become. I think if Sydney had been gold, it would have cancelled out Atlanta completely. Erased it. If I had done that, then Athens would not have been so final.

If I could go back and change things, I would go back and change Sydney rather than Atlanta – but that is using Sydney to wipe out Atlanta, I suppose!

At the end of this story which has no real ending, am I a success or a failure?

I suppose, overall, a success; but I think I could have achieved more. That could just be me and my curse never to be satisfied! Many people I speak to would tell me that, if they had achieved half of what I did, they would be happy. But it depends on whether you know there was more and better in you. Athletically, I feel fulfilled.

I do think there is something else for me to do in life. There is something I need to do outside of running. Until I find that, then I won't see running in its proper place. It's not a running thing, or an athletics thing. It is an all-round thing. It is me as a person. It could be motherhood. It could be making the decision to live somewhere. It could be doing something with my life, like becoming a primary school teacher. I'm at the crossroads.

At the end of it all, am I as happy as I thought I would be? I don't know if anybody would be happier. Any adventure ends. Does anyone have the perfect ending? For a few years now I have been trying to find this fairytale ending, pick a goal, set a target, achieve that and draw a line under it.

Life isn't like that, though. It's not a kid's book. I can't choose my ending. I have tried marathons, the European Cross Country, the Commonwealth Games. They could have been the 'happy ever after', but none of them really worked out. I'm still looking for chances to get that ending. Dublin 2009? Who knows?

Generally now I am happy. When I don't have to think about running I am happy. There are things which are unanswered, even to me they are unanswered. I just move on. It is very easy to achieve something and make yourself happy by getting something. It is hard to describe that feeling. Generally on a day-to-day basis, doing stuff with the kids and being busy, I am quite happy doing all that. That is achievement.

Right now my goal is just to stay fit. That keeps me happy enough. I'm an all-or-nothing person. If I get a run in, I can do anything. What have I learned? Life isn't a fairytale. It doesn't just offer you the fairytale ending. You make it happen. The trick is to keep moving and hope you are in a fairytale sort of place when the great race stops and somebody else writes the ending.

Acknowledgements

I would particularly like to thank Tom Humphries and Penguin Ireland for helping me to put this story on to paper. It has been running around in my head for a long time now, and to finally get it down in ink is all credit to the encouragement I got from Penguin Ireland and the time and energy put in by Tom. The teamwork was great: Tom listened, I spoke. It was all there on tape and finally, after many months of writing and reading and taps on the shoulder, here is a book that I am proud to call *My Story*. The cover photo was the easy part, and for this I can thank my good friend, Patrick Bolger . . . choosing the picture was another matter.

This story could not be told without all the people who have touched me at one time or another in my life. You all know who you are, and you also know that it is too long a list to include here. To everyone who has ever written a letter or a card to me: they have all been received and appreciated on so many occasions. You have all been on this rollercoaster ride with me, thank you for making the effort to share your thoughts with me.

My parents, John and Mary, my sister Gillian and brother Tony, for always being there for me through all the ups and downs, for dealing with the intrusions into your privacy at times when I could just run away and hide.

Nic, the most positive person in my life, your patience and willpower never cease to amaze me; thanks for sharing so much with me, for showing me the light at the end of the tunnel over and over again, and for taking the chance to jump on this rollercoaster ride through life with me.

In memory of my Aunt Fran Shealy, your kindness and friendship are a great loss to all who knew you.

Index